The Outstanding Middle Manager

The Outstanding Middle Manager

How to be a healthy, happy,
high-performing mid-level manager

Gordon Tinline and Cary Cooper

Kogan Page

LONDON PHILADELPHIA NEW DELHI

First published in Great Britain and the United States in 2016 by Kogan Page Limited

2nd Floor, 45 Gee Street	1518 Walnut Street, Suite 900	4737/23 Ansari Road
London EC1V 3RS	Philadelphia PA 19102	Daryaganj
United Kingdom	USA	New Delhi 110002
		India

www.koganpage.com

© Gordon Tinline and Cary Cooper, 2016

The right of Gordon Tinline and Cary Cooper to be identified as the authors of this work has been asserted by them in accordance with the Copyright, Designs and Patents Act 1988.

ISBN   978 0 7494 7466 9
E-ISBN 978 0 7494 7467 6

British Library Cataloguing-in-Publication Data

A CIP record for this book is available from the British Library.

Library of Congress Cataloging-in-Publication Data

Names: Tinline, Gordon, author.
Title: The outstanding middle manager : how to be a healthy, happy,
   high-performing mid-level manager / Gordon Tinline, Cary Cooper.
Description: 1st Edition. | Philadelphia, PA : Kogan Page, 2016. | Includes
   bibliographical references and index.
Identifiers: LCCN 2016028095 (print) | LCCN 2016034755 (ebook) | ISBN
   9780749474669 (paperback) | ISBN 9780749474676 (eISBN) |
Subjects: LCSH: Management. | Leadership. | BISAC: BUSINESS & ECONOMICS /
   Management. | BUSINESS & ECONOMICS / Leadership. | PSYCHOLOGY / Industrial
   & Organizational Psychology.
Classification: LCC HD31.2 .T56 2016 (print) | LCC HD31.2 (ebook) | DDC
   658.4/09–dc23
LC record available at https://lccn.loc.gov/2016028095

Typeset by SPi Global
Print production managed by Jellyfish
Printed and bound by CPI Group (UK) Ltd, Croydon, CR0 4YY

CONTENTS

Life in the middle

01

In this chapter we set the scene for our take on middle management. We cover the important background and context relating to the changing role for those operating in what is often a canyon between the shop floor/first line management levels and senior management. We emphasize that while the title 'middle manager' is no longer prevalent, many people still undertake middle management as a core part of their role.

We provide an introduction to the major themes that are woven through the fabric of this book. These include:

- The reality of life in the middle, particularly in terms of the pressures faced.

- The need for a positive reframing of middle management activity and the importance of resilience for those that populate this space.

- The changing nature of power and influence from a mid-level hierarchical position, including important cross-cultural issues.

- The need to take a whole-person perspective on managing in the middle.

The chapter concludes with a practical tool for starting to capture your goals if you are managing in the middle. This uses a structure that maps onto the content of the book and which you can build upon as you read through it.

You sit somewhere in the middle in your organization's hierarchy. You have progressed beyond first, and perhaps second, line management. You're not at executive level but you may well report to someone who is. So how's life? It's quite likely you feel that you are constantly in a work pressure sandwich with frequent demands from above and below. You may well be trying to understand what your development path is and stay motivated about further progressing your career. Life pressures away from work could be significant and you may be struggling to manage the cross-over between work and the rest of your life. This begins to build into quite a depressing scenario, but life in the middle doesn't have to be this way.

Let's paint an alternative picture. You can see across your organization, above, below and all around you. This puts you in a position where you can have an impact and influence in all directions. You have a myriad of developmental options in your organization. Your life is rich and varied and you can blend your work into the rest of your life in a way that enhances both. This isn't utopia. It is achievable but often requires us to radically rethink life in the middle and, just as challengingly, change our habits and behaviour.

It's unrealistic to suggest that we can create a perfect world. There will be times when life in the middle is difficult and stressful. However, we need to start by ensuring we avoid a state of learned helplessness. Seligman defines this state as 'the giving-up reaction, the quitting response that follows from the belief that whatever you do doesn't matter' (Seligman, 2006: 15). Working with a wide range of mid-level people in businesses and organizations we frequently see signs of learned helplessness. For example, we often hear middle managers say that they feel they cannot do anything because they are completely overloaded. However, there is plenty of evidence, which we will outline later, that other factors such as the level of perceived control people have or the extent to which they feel supported can be just as important as workload for determining effectiveness. This is a classic situation where facing extreme pressure in one area can feel overpowering to the point that we no longer believe we can make a significant difference in any area of our life. If this is how you frequently feel then this book can help you to avoid this state. We will develop this mainly in Chapter 3, which focuses on managing pressures in the middle.

A key objective of this book is to help people reframe their experience of life in the middle. It is targeted at those who undertake middle management activity rather than explicitly middle managers. This may seem a subtle distinction but it is an important one. It is based on our view that while few have the job title 'middle manager', many undertake middle management as a core part of their role. This book is mainly written for those who manage managers but are below board or executive level. This includes those who may have fairly senior roles in large businesses with substantial responsibility and span of control, such as divisional or departmental heads. It will also be relevant for senior specialists, where the role becomes not just being an expert but a manager and leader of experts. The book is focused on *life* in the middle, not technical or functional skills. If you are looking to improve your budgeting or project management skills, you won't find areas like this directly addressed. However, you should find guidance that helps you in all areas of middle management life.

Historically the view of the middle manager has been far from positive. Back in 1990 a typical middle manager was profiled as 'a frustrated, disillusioned individual caught in the middle of a hierarchy, impotent and with no real hope for career progression' (Dopson and Stewart, 1990). In fact, management activity generally seems to have become progressively less fashionable in the past two or three decades, particularly in comparison to leadership. We are not setting out to argue that being a middle manager should be held up as the pinnacle of achievement or the ultimate aspiration. Rather, we suggest that middle management as an area of functional activity is important and forms a large part of the day-to-day role played by many people in organizations. We also argue that middle management development has been somewhat neglected and that this has negative implications for those in mid-level roles and the wider organization.

The demise of middle management has been predicted by many over the last few decades (eg Gratton, 2012). Yet in 2012 the *Wall Street Journal* estimated there were 10.8 million middle managers in the United States, making up nearly 8 per cent of the total workforce. This represented a rise of close to 2 per cent of the US workforce from 10 years previously. Numbers do ebb and flow with economic conditions and vary by sector. What is clear is that middle management roles are changing as a result of technological, commercial and generational influences. For example, the rise of the knowledge worker economy is one change that is redefining the role of middle management (Bañares Parera and Fernández-Vallejo, 2013). We will consider the nature of these changes and their implications for developing your career in the middle of organizations in Chapter 4.

At the end of this chapter there is a simple tool to help you clarify your goals in relation to managing in the middle. These might be related to managing the pressure you experience better, developing your career more effectively, lifestyle management, or influencing and getting the best out of your team and colleagues. You are encouraged to use this to direct your learning and get the most from the contents of this book. In the final chapter we will focus on consolidating and taking forward what you have learnt from this book. To help you capture your goals let's consider some background that should aid your thinking about the areas we cover and your priorities.

What is the reality of life in the middle?

Let's start fairly generally with life satisfaction. Most readers are likely to be in a broad age band from mid-30s to mid-60s. Looking at data from across Europe, life satisfaction seems to be lower in this age band than it is for younger or older people (European Commission, 2013). These data also reveal that the highest stress age band, by a considerable way, is 35–49-year olds. In addition, key protective factors for reducing stress may well be less than optimal for many busy people in the middle of organizations. For example, job security is very likely to have become weaker for many in recent times. When you combine this with other protective factors that may well be threatened, such as avoiding excessive debt, maintaining physical activity and strong family and friend networks, it is not difficult to build a high risk profile for many at busy mid-career and life stages. Of course this does not mean that lower life satisfaction in your middle years is certain but it does highlight that there is a trend; suggesting it is more likely unless you actively work to mitigate the risks.

So life satisfaction is likely to be lower for those in their middle years. What about stress levels for those in mid-level positions? A UK survey of 6,000 employees across a range of industries and levels highlighted that stress levels were particularly high for middle managers (BUPA, 2013), with one in five reporting feeling stressed for over a year. One implication of this was that managers felt unable to support more junior staff. Workload was found to be the greatest perceived stressor. There is additional research from the US, based on a sample of nearly 22,000 workers, which indicates that those in mid-level roles in organizations are the most prone to anxiety and depression (Prins *et al*, 2015). The authors of this work hypothesize that a combination of responsibility, workload and power dynamics might explain this.

Generational differences provide useful insights in building a picture of mid-career and life. It is a reasonable assumption that at the time of the publication of this book most people in the middle of organizations are Gen X (born mid-1960s to mid-1980s), with some Boomers (born post-World War II to mid-1960s) and Gen Y (born mid-1980s to 2000). The stress profile for Gen X is probably representative of many in the middle. The American Psychological Society in its annual *Stress in America* report (APA, 2014) highlights some relevant Gen X issues. This work shows that one key area where Gen X tend to fare poorly in comparison to younger and older people is in the amount and quality of sleep they typically get. As well as having health implications, lack of sleep is increasingly linked with poor decision making quality and work performance problems. Regular lack of sleep can leave you in a state of heightened reactivity. Interestingly, this has an impact on your reaction to both negative and positive events (Gujar *et al*, 2011). This can leave you in a see-saw state where you react very negatively when something goes wrong and amazingly positively when something goes right. This is potentially very exhausting for you and your colleagues; a kind of hyper-reactive state where you are thrown to extremes and certainly not well-equipped to make balanced decisions. Does this sound like you or any of your colleagues?

One reality that is changing life in the middle relates to career progression and development. As organizations flatten and broaden with often blurred boundaries, the emphasis shifts to developing your career laterally and qualitatively rather than a more traditional focus on the next promotion. There has also been a shift towards individuals taking responsibility for their own career development and progression rather than the organization setting out a clear structure and pathway. This appears to be true across cultures in the developed world. For example, Hassard *et al* (2012) found that this reality was similar in the United Kingdom, United States and Japan.

Taking these three areas together – life satisfaction, stress and career development – it is clear that life in the middle of organizations is challenging. It is not difficult to see how many could become demotivated, unhealthy and believe that all they have to look forward to is retirement. However, there are plenty of reasons for optimism. The time seems right to try to reframe how middle management is viewed, by those populating this space as well as others. As organizations continue to flatten, the middle is the place where many will spend the majority of their career. Others have noted the importance of middle management strategically (Currie and Procter, 2005; Floyd and Woodridge, 1994). In the last decade, major management consultancies such as Boston Consulting Group (2010) and Accenture (2007) have argued there is a need for stronger middle management. So we need to find a new positive future for those seeking to not only manage but thrive in the middle of modern organizations.

A positive view of middle management

There is very little doubt that to survive and thrive in the middle you actively need to manage a range of pressures and work to create a positive trajectory for yourself. One perspective that is very useful in starting to define how we can make this a reality is to focus on psychological resilience. We regularly work with a wide range of businesses and public sector organizations to build psychological resilience in individuals and teams, and many of the people we meet are trying to manage in the middle.

Resilience is the capacity to maintain your wellbeing and work performance under pressure and to recover well when you face a setback. One researcher whose work we often draw on here is Dennis Charney, a psychiatrist and neurobiologist based at New York's Mount Sinai Icahn School of Medicine. With his co-workers Charney has developed a Resilience Prescription (Southwick and Charney, 2012) and we will use elements of this in Chapter 3 to explore how we can best deal with the pressures of middle management in both the short and long term. One aspect within this that is worth introducing early is the need to be able to reframe events that are having a negative impact on us. In many ways, as already stated, we need to start by reframing how we see middle management.

Reframing requires us to be aware of and challenge our thoughts and beliefs. So what thoughts and beliefs about life in the middle might be common and unhelpful? Here are two that we regularly encounter: 1) middle managers are blockers, they are resistant to change and deliberately make it difficult to implement; and 2) bureaucracy is largely created by middle managers.

The first stage in challenging such beliefs is to probe to find out what real evidence there is that supports them. Perhaps in doing so you'd discover that occasionally it's not middle managers who are barriers to change so much as that the rationale and drivers for change haven't been articulated properly from the top. Could it be that change is difficult to implement in the middle as that is where workloads are highest and there are a dozen new initiatives requiring attention at the same time? Perhaps the middle is where the strategic ideas from senior management meet the reality of implementation for the front line, which means adapting old systems of work and creating new ones – and this ends up being labelled 'bureaucracy'. Once you start to challenge some of the common assumptions and stereotypes about middle management it is relatively easy to expose the lack of evidence behind many of them. From that point onwards, alternative conceptualizations can be developed.

The problem is we often tend to accept common views of middle management without challenging them frequently enough. This can create a self-fulfilling negative reality. Confirmation bias is a well-established thinking bias or heuristic: having accepted a notion we then pay attention almost exclusively to the evidence that supports it. There is a strong likelihood that many of the ideas that are well entrenched regarding middle management have been heavily influenced by confirmation bias, as well as other thinking errors.

Another important aspect of maintaining and building resilience is the capacity to understand and play to your strengths. It is very easy to get drawn into lengthy negative spirals of behaviour where you begin to wonder if you have any strengths at all. Often HR processes such as performance appraisals serve more to reinforce the need to correct weaknesses than to build on and develop strengths. At mid-levels in organizations you are likely to have a set of development needs that has been driven by years of appraisals. How many of those development needs are strengths? Working with a wide range of managers at various levels we frequently find that their development needs are dominated by weaknesses, or are exclusively compiled from them. These are aspects of working behaviour and activity that they are naturally weak in and have usually been battling to improve for a long time. If this characterizes your development needs and objectives then you are striving to be average, at best. Identifying and developing strengths is much more likely to unlock new potential and you will feel much better than when you are constantly trying to improve in your weakest areas.

Strengths thinking has been strongly informed by ideas from positive psychology in recent years. The positive emotional spiral that can result is worth more than just feeling good – although there is nothing wrong with that as a goal in itself. Fredrickson *et al* (2008) demonstrate this well with their 'broaden and build' approach. This argues that positive emotional experience can open out our thinking (broaden), leading to better problem-solving and coping strategies that ultimately further enhance positive emotions (build). Understanding and playing to your strengths is much more likely to unlock such a spiral than constantly being dragged down into negative, weakness-dominated behavioural cycles. We are not arguing that you should ignore your weaknesses but rather that your development orientation should be weighted towards strengths.

Don't tell anyone, but you may be a middle manager

As noted above, very few people have 'middle manager' as their job title. The popular New York-based professional job-matching site,

The Ladders, analysed job titles in 2013 and noted that the title of 'manager' was on the slide while specialist titles were on the rise (The Ladders, 2013). However, if you sit between first-level supervision and senior executive levels then middle management activity is likely to be a major part of your role. There has been a shift away from explicit generalist middle manager roles and that shift has occurred in two main ways. The first change is the rise of the senior specialist and the second is the stronger focus on leadership rather than management. Let's briefly consider both of these and their implications.

The Ladders analysis highlighted some of the fastest growing job titles in the last five years. In the main these were specialist titles such as 'Data scientist', 'Staff accountant' and 'Android developer'. In all probability as people in these roles get promoted they will have the word 'Senior' placed in front of their job title, and then progress to become 'Head of...'. They will then find themselves asked to undertake management activity as well as continuing to lead through their specialist knowledge base. In some ways, rather than move from specialist to generalist, it is much more likely that you will move to specialist *plus* generalist. This can mean you find yourself with two roles when you thought you were just being recognized as a lead specialist. If this has been your journey you will have had to adapt to being a leader of experts, rather than just an expert and, with further advancement, to core middle management activity such as resourcing and budgeting. At the same time, you may well be expected to still be a knowledge leader or guru in your specialist area.

There is very little doubt that leadership has become much more popular than management. Leadership development is seen as forward looking and dynamic while traditional management development has become unfashionable and boring. The difference between leadership and management is usually characterized as the former being concerned with direction and inspiring and the latter with processes and control. While leadership development programmes have become ubiquitous they often appear to retain large components of management development and occasionally the two terms are used interchangeably without adequate definition. For example, take a prestigious programme such as the Harvard Business School Executive

Education Program for Leadership Development. It has the attractive strap line 'Accelerating the Careers of High Potential Leaders'. However, it then goes on to state a core benefit thus:

> Its comprehensive and holistic approach broadens your understanding of core business functions and deepens your confidence to take on greater cross-functional responsibility. With a broader grasp of management and greater confidence, you will return to your company with a personal action plan for identifying and addressing the key challenges facing your organization. (Harvard Business School, 2015)

Now this reads as much like traditional middle management territory as it does cutting-edge dynamic leadership. Of course this could just be confusing marketing. However, it may well illustrate that to some extent we are still developing management but under the cloak of the more popular leadership label. In reality when you are in the middle in most organizations you will need to both lead and manage. It is the activities that really matter, not the labels. We will expand upon these key activities and their implications throughout this book without getting too concerned at every juncture about whether we are focusing on leadership or management.

Power and influence

Do you feel you have the power and influence you need in your role? Can you influence what and whom you need to sufficiently to enable you to meet your objectives? Of course power and influence are not the same. We will mainly be concerned with influence in this book and how it can be successfully exerted from the middle, in all directions. However, it is worth considering the nature of power in modern organizations. Understanding and classifying sources of power in organizations has a long history. For example, French and Raven (1960) identified five sources, or bases, of organizational power over half a century ago. Let's review a couple of these in terms of how they may be experienced in the middle of modern organizations: reward and expert power.

Reward power

In our work with a number of businesses and public sector organizations we have often been struck by the variation among managers at the same level in the same organization in the reward power they believe they have. Many feel they have very limited power here with reward structures being determined and fixed by the centre and with power lying between senior management and HR. However, a number of their colleagues have often challenged this and as a result discovered they have more discretion over the rewards their people receive than they thought. The nature of these rewards may not be direct salary enhancements but perhaps in other forms such as one-off bonuses or life experiences such as vouchers for leisure activities. This again exemplifies learned helplessness, with many slipping into a belief system along the lines of 'That's just the way it is' without challenging the constraints they are convinced they are shackled by. Of course the other consideration here is the nature of reward. Thinking only in narrow monetary terms is probably a limiting factor in its own right. Rewards in the shape of new opportunities and of course genuine expressions of thanks are often within the power of managers even when monetary discretion is tightly constrained. These may be more motivational in the long term than solely monetary reward.

Expert power

Expert power plays out in complex ways in many organizations. On the one hand, as noted above, we have seen the rise of the senior specialist, which can lead to powerful individuals in terms of expertise. However, counteracting this has been the increasing emphasis on knowledge management combined with ever-more sophisticated platforms for collaborative working. The goals of such changes are usually to ensure expertise is distributed and that business-critical knowledge and skill does not reside only in the brains of a few talented experts. Arguably this does not diminish expert power but changes the nature of it. Expertise for, say, a head of research and development in a large business is as much about how to exploit knowledge and manage innovation as it is about being an expert in a narrow technical or scientific area. There is also a strong need to know when to collaborate in an open source manner and when to fiercely protect knowledge collateral and intellectual property.

Power dynamics vary across national cultures. A well-established concept that helps us to understand power across cultures is Hofstede's 'power distance' (Hofstede, 2001). This refers to the extent to which people accept that power in organizations and institutions is distributed unequally. In a high power distance country, such as Malaysia, people tend to readily accept hierarchical status differences and expect deferential respect to be shown accordingly. In a low power distance country, for example Denmark, people tend to be less concerned with organizational rank and hierarchical expectations. In the middle of organizations this will have real implications for the most effective way to use power and influence. Managers working globally need to be aware of such differences and adjust their style appropriately. For example, a participative open management approach is often held up as being optimal in most Western countries. However, this has been shown to be related to lower profitability in businesses in high power distance countries, such as many in Asia (Newman and Nollen, 1996). Power distance seems to have been relatively stable in many countries, but those that have experienced major socio-political change in recent decades (eg Eastern European countries) have seen some real shifts, mainly towards a lowering of power distance (Taras *et al*, 2012).

Power is clearly still relevant in modern organizations, particularly if you operate globally, but its nature has changed dramatically since the early theorists developed their categorizations and models. In many ways influence rather than power has become much more important. As structures flatten and hierarchical power diminishes, the ability to influence without a strong formal power base becomes essential. Many organizations adopt matrix-like structures and this further amplifies the need for influencing skills as the distribution of formal power is complex and diffuse. In Chapters 5 to 7 we will focus on how we can influence upwards, downwards and sideways from a strong middle position. This is where being in the middle can give you a unique source of power through the influence you can exert. We will seek to help you do this more effectively later in this book.

All of you

One core perspective we take is the 'whole person' one. Just focusing on who you are and what you do in your working life would be artificial and inadequate. It is obvious that the pressures you experience at work can have an impact on the rest of your life, and vice versa. Many businesses have operated on the basis that their only concern is what happens with their employees at work and what they do in the workplace. Work and non-work pressures have often been separated by organizations as if they affected different people. In particular, there is often a reluctance to intervene when an employee is experiencing significant non-work problems. In most countries the organization's duty of care to its employees is understandably bounded by the contracted working environment. However, there are two compelling reasons for taking a whole-person perspective and considering both work and non-work pressures: 1) non-work pressures account for a significant proportion of stress and mental health-related problems in the workplace (eg sickness absence, support required from Employee Assistance Programmes, employee turnover); and 2) non-work pressures are likely to interact with work pressures in a way that could increase the likelihood of behavioural and performance-related problems manifesting in the workplace.

These aspects are just as relevant for those in the middle in organizations as they are at more junior and senior levels. In fact, there may be reasons to believe that they are more pertinent at middle levels than elsewhere. For example, those in middle management roles are quite likely to be part of the 'sandwich generation': those who end up having caring responsibilities for both children and aging parents simultaneously (Roots, 1998). You may be feeling the pressures of being in the middle both at work and in your family life. As people live longer and the cost of care escalates it is likely that the sandwich generation will continue to grow in numbers. This will be most relevant for women in mid-level organizational positions as they are much more likely than men to carry the heaviest caring burden. In practice many researchers interested in this area define the sandwich generation as women with dual parental and child caring responsibilities. Some recent research we were involved with, undertaken in the UK financial services sector, showed that while sandwich generation individuals can often maintain their productivity levels it is their health that really suffers (Smeed and Tinline, 2014).

In middle management roles you are likely to be able to do much of your work whenever you chose to, regardless of location. This can make balancing work demands with those in the rest of your life very challenging. We often talk about work-life balance but we find this term can be misleading as it tends to suggest that one force has to pull against the other. A more useful way to think about this is work-life integration. Does work fit into the rest of your life in a way that is productive, healthy and sustainable? This will vary depending on a number of factors such as the nature of your work and indeed your personality (Wayne *et al*, 2004). Some people integrate their work well into their life overall and don't need a fixed boundary between the two, whereas others struggle with this approach and operate best by keeping the two domains as separate as possible.

The other main reason for taking a whole-person approach is the need to consider all aspects of wellbeing, physical as well as psychological. For example, the impact of your physical condition on your psychological capacity to cope well with pressure is clear. In particular, the importance of regular exercise for positive mental health now has a well-established evidence base (Penedo and Dahn, 2005). Establishing and maintaining healthy lifestyle habits has to be a core part of your strategy for surviving and thriving in a demanding mid-level career. We will expand on the relevant life management aspects in Chapter 8 with the objective of offering useful, well-grounded, practical strategies.

Establish your goals and objectives

We hope that this book helps you make the most of your career and life if you are somewhere in the middle of an organizational hierarchy. We believe it will be a useful resource for those whose role is to support the development and performance of those in mid-level positions. Our key objectives are to help you to:

- develop a more positive and holistic perspective on being a middle manager/senior specialist;

- enhance the skills and approach you need to operate effectively as a middle manager;

- become more strategic in your approach to mid-career development, recognizing the options open to forging a more fulfilling and varied career, even when opportunities for vertical progression are limited;

- become more resilient, better equipped to manage pressure, with focused strategies for optimal work-life integration.

This chapter has provided some background on life in the middle and introduced the key themes that are relevant to the above objectives. We will expand upon these themes in the following chapters. In the next chapter we will build the context for life in middle management by considering the perspectives of those at more senior and junior levels. The book includes a number of practical tools that should help you apply the learning you gain from it. This includes the one below, which is intended to help you clarify your goals in reading this book. At this stage these goals may be broad and not very well defined. The fact that they are not yet fully formed is not a problem, and in fact it may be a positive in that you have an open approach to further developing your goals as you progress through the content of the book.

When considering your goals, you are encouraged to make them challenging. Stretch goals, scary as they often seem when you capture them, are more likely to lift your level of performance and attainment (Latham, 2004). Start by considering what you think your life in the middle would need to be like to maximize your positive feelings and provide you with a strong sense of purpose. Aim high: there is no need to self-impose limits based on what you believe is achievable at this stage, or perhaps at any stage!

DEVELOPMENT TOOL

Managing in the middle: defining your goals

Goal setting is one of the best established and most effective ways of motivating yourself and others (Locke, 1984). Figure 1.1 is intended to help you map your goals for managing in the middle. It sets out four areas to help you structure and capture your goals as they relate to the focus and objectives of this book.

Figure 1.1 Managing in the middle: goal capture framework

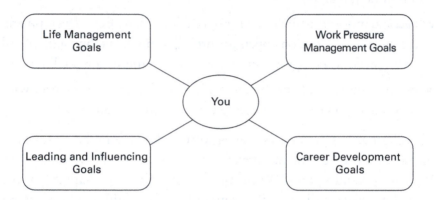

- Work pressure management goals (Chapter 3) – what are your goals for reducing stress at work and ensuring you can focus on important priorities and challenges and not be drawn into negative hindrance spirals?

- Career development goals (Chapter 4) – career development does not need to be founded on hierarchical advancement. There are many ways to develop your career without promotion. What would you like to achieve in your career and why is this important to you?

- Leading and influencing goals (Chapters 5, 6 and 7) – what would you like to achieve by influencing your colleagues more effectively? Consider influencing upwards (senior management) and sideways (peers). What would you like to achieve with your team or those who directly report to you?

- Life management goals (Chapter 8) – what do you want to improve in your life away from work, and what is important to help you to integrate work into your whole life more effectively?

To get the most from this book you are encouraged to capture your thoughts on your goals in these areas at this stage. As you read the most relevant chapters you should revisit and refine your goals.

Below we provide some specific prompts that should help you think about and capture your goals. Try to be as specific as possible. Don't worry too much about how ambitious or obtainable these appear to be at this stage; tilt towards stretching rather than easily obtainable goals for now. You can hone and develop them as you progress through the book. In each area try to capture both your goals and your thoughts on the benefits of achieving them.

Work pressure management goals

(Revisit after reading Chapter 3.)

- What would make you feel less stressed at work?

- What are your challenge pressures (these will be difficult but you associate them with positive outcomes or learning)?

- What are the main activities that drain your energy at work; how can you avoid or better manage these?

- Think about: demands and workload; how much control and influence you feel you have; resource pressures; relationships at work; change; your key responsibilities.

Career development goals

(Revisit after reading Chapter 4.)

- What would success in your career look like without further promotion?

- What kind of work do you enjoy most? How could you expand your opportunities for engaging in this kind of work?

- What opportunities are there to undertake a wider range of, or different, responsibilities at the level you are at?

- What rewards motivate you best? (Don't just think about money!)

Leading and influencing goals

(Revisit after reading Chapters 5, 6 and 7.)

- What would you like to achieve with your team?

- How would you like to influence your boss more effectively?

- What would having a bigger positive impact on your peers at the same level as you look and feel like?

- How would you like to be regarded by your colleagues?

Life management goals

(Revisit after reading Chapter 8.)

- What brings joy to your life? Do you spend enough time on these activities?

- What do you really need to feel happy and healthy?

- Does your work fit well into the rest of your life? What would make this easier or better?

- Do you have healthy lifestyle habits (eg regular exercise, good sleep patterns, and limited alcohol consumption)? What would you most like to change in this regard?

Life above and below 02

In this chapter we explore the reality of working life for those at more senior and junior levels in organizations. We argue that understanding their perspectives is crucial to functioning effectively in middle management. We consider both the experience of those at the top and those at more junior levels. At the top we discuss strategic drivers, interpersonal dynamics and the personal motivations of those at the most senior level. At lower levels we use a wellbeing and performance model to reflect on three key aspects: control and autonomy, job security and change, and work relationships.

The chapter concludes with a process tool for helping those in the middle better understand the perspective of their colleagues at more senior and junior levels.

To fully understand life in the middle of an organization it is necessary to consider what life is like for those at the top and those at lower levels. In our experience many people fail to develop an appreciation of the perspective of those at different levels than their own. The result can be at best an inaccurate perception of others, and at worst form the basis of poor communication and engagement between different levels. Having a well-developed understanding of life at different levels in organizations provides a platform for positive relationships, more effective and productive working, and successful change. Without this we may well blunder on in our own little world without recognizing the impact our actions have on others and ultimately how well we will be able to work with them.

So this chapter is all about perspectives: the reality for those around you in your business or organization and how this shapes your reality. Of course you may well have been promoted within your organization and therefore will have your own lived experience of more junior roles. This can be useful, but it is also important to recognize that the path an individual takes through an organization, particularly a large and complex one, is one route among many.

Let's start by considering the reality of life at the top in organizations and by extension what that means for those in the middle. How's your relationship with your manager? There is evidence that this can have as large an impact on your working experience as any other single factor. One finding often cited over the last 15 years is based on Gallup's analysis of 25 years' worth of US survey data, which concluded that people leave managers rather than companies (Buckingham and Coffman, 1999). While this has been challenged to some extent, most of us recognize how important the relationship with the boss is to our working life. Therefore, understanding his or her perspective can be enormously important for your effectiveness and wellbeing. It's not just what your boss thinks of you directly, it is his or her wider pressures and outlook that will have a day-to-day impact on your experience with him or her. There are three core aspects that we will expand upon to help us understand the reality of life at, or very close to, the top in organizations:

- *Strategic drivers* – what drives people at the top in terms of their strategic pressures and ambitions and how this can cascade through the organization.

- *Interpersonal dynamics* – relationships at the top and with those in the middle, including key power and political factors.

- *Personal motivations* – the personal goals and ambitions of your boss and how they are likely to have an impact on you.

Strategic drivers at the top

One thing you can be certain of is that senior executives and leaders will be required to have and hone a clear strategy. If you work in a large public limited company or corporation this will be magnified by external shareholder demands constantly insisting that the business has a leading-edge competitive strategy. This rarely results in a steady state for any length of time. The senior execs' reward for devising and leading well strategically is often increased demands to revise and improve their last strategy. This means that they will frequently be under unrelenting pressure to design and lead wave after wave of change. This isn't unique to businesses with external shareholders. For example, public sector organizations are increasingly expected to change strategically in the face of tighter public purses, including pressure to change the organizational culture. This is particularly true in many developed countries with mature public sectors including the United Kingdom (CIPD, 2012; Schofield, 2008), France (Migeon, 2011) and Australia (Bajkowski, 2015). This often comes with partisan political motivations and interference.

We frequently find in our work in organizations that repeated waves of strategic change can create strong cynicism at middle and lower levels. This is often most evident when there is a change of chief executive or at the very top of the organization. The expectation is that the new man, or unfortunately less frequently woman, will need to completely change things to ensure they make their mark. Obviously this can be driven by the personal ambition of the new head (more on that below) but it is not difficult to see that anyone appointed to lead a large organization is very unlikely to get away with saying, 'I'll just do the same as the last guy!'

Senior executives will expect those who report to them to engage with them in the continuous process of strategic change and innovation. If you sit one or two levels from the top you are likely to meet the twin demands to think and engage strategically and also lead the tactical implementation of major change programmes. Depending on your level of involvement in the strategy formation process it is also possible that from time to time you will be asked to implement programmes you may not fully understand the rationale for, or that you completely understand but disagree with. This can be extremely challenging, particularly when those who report to you are trying to evaluate whether you truly buy into a change programme and are bombarding you with scores of questions you don't have the answers to. Chapter 7 expands on approaches for managing upwards and this includes ways of clarifying and improving your role in implementing change.

Interpersonal dynamics

When you are somewhere in the middle it is easy to get caught in the crossfire of senior level politics and power plays. To understand this we should start by being clear on what we mean by power and politics in an organizational context. This quote from Jeffrey Pfeffer (1992) captures it in a way that is still relevant today:

> Power is... the potential ability to influence behaviour, to change the course of events, to overcome resistance, and to get people to do things they would not otherwise do. Politics and influence are the processes, the actions, the behaviours through which this potential power is utilized and realized. (p 45)

When there is a power struggle at the top, like seismic waves the closer you are to the epicentre the more powerful the impact. When this happens you need to decide what or whom to hold onto to survive the turmoil. You need to decide quickly where your loyalties lie, but that doesn't have to be solely to one individual, even if this is your manager. It may be that what helps you survive senior power struggles, and possibly even improve your status, is constancy of purpose rather than blind loyalty to a person. Understanding your own values and purpose serves you well when there are power plays above and around you: it's an anchor through the storm. This can also help you play a role that is ultimately respected by those on opposing ends of a power struggle. Of course you may be accused of trying to sit on the fence and of refusing to commit. However, sometimes hedging your bets and keeping your options open for as long as possible is the best approach. There are a broader range of reasons why understanding your core purpose is important and these are developed further later in the book in terms of managing pressure (Chapter 3) and career development (Chapter 4). In this context it's about supporting your decision making when there are power plays around, and particularly above, you. It is also ultimately about the reputation you develop regarding your reactions when facing interpersonal turbulence; to paraphrase Kipling, keeping your head when all about you are losing theirs.

It's not all about power, although having an awareness of the nature of this and the power bases and plays at work above you is important. Sometimes you can get caught up in conflicts and disagreements at senior levels that are based on either policy or personality. The former are probably easier to deal with by taking a rational approach and seeking to understand the basis of the conflict. You may also be able to play a helpful role in finding ground where compromise between opposing policy positions is feasible. This is also where the benefit of being closer to policy implementation than more senior executives or leaders can be an advantage. Offering your perspective on policy implementation regularly may be valued strongly by more senior leaders. We regularly hear people at middle to lower levels in organizations respond to policy and structural change initiatives with the words, 'They just haven't thought it through.' Those in mid-level roles can play a critical role in helping 'them' think it through.

To some extent this perception reveals a broader issue about change expectations and the reality of implementing strategic change. In our view this is often a manifestation of a deeper view, which is the less frequently expressed: 'They haven't thought through what it means for my job!' This is usually true. Strategic, top-led change is driven by competitive pressures and organizational size and shape issues. The implementation of this through a large and complex organization requires co-creation at all levels. This is only successful with truly empowered workforces and open and mature relationships. This is a theme we will return to below and in later chapters. Providing honest and pertinent feedback upwards is a skill that we will develop in Chapter 7.

Perhaps the most difficult interpersonal fall-out to deal with is when there is a personality clash at the top level in a business or organization. This can result in blood on the carpet. These clashes usually lead to problems further down that are difficult to counter with rational responses. Of course senior leaders have a responsibility to their organizations not to allow personality clashes to derail effectiveness. Nevertheless, there are documented examples of where such clashes have been extremely destructive. For example, a senior executive at Disney, commenting on the personality clash a decade ago between the then President and CEO of the company, publicly stated: 'This was two big volatile egos banging against each other and they just didn't get along' (Stanley P Gold, quoted in Knowledge@ Wharton, 2005). The result of this was that the Disney President, Michael Ovitz, left the company after 14 months with a $140 million severance package and severe disruption to the business. Arguably the reason such cases grab the headlines is that they are relatively infrequent. There are those that argue that extreme personality types, possibly even bordering on the psychotic, are disproportionately frequently found at senior levels (eg Wellons, 2012). If this is the case then dysfunctional relationships at this level may be more frequent and damaging than at other levels.

So senior level personality clashes probably occur from time to time with negative consequences. If you are sitting under these storms you can expect to get wet. Do you just take shelter and wait until the climate improves or do you get involved? This probably depends on how long you think the storm will last. If there is a dysfunctional relationship above you and there is little evidence of it improving, or of one of the protagonists leaving, you will need a strategy to deal with it. This might mean openly siding with one party, which is likely to be particularly tempting if your manager is involved. Recognizing that this is a choice and possibly a high risk one is important. Alternatively, you may seek to maintain a level of impartiality. In the long term this is often the best position to take. Nevertheless the pressure to take sides can be difficult to resist. One approach that may help is to frequently use a questioning mode to seek to clarify how different parties view each other and perhaps play a role in bridging their divide to some degree. An approach for doing this, and handling similar conflicts at a senior level, is outlined in Chapter 7.

Personal motivations

Senior people in organizations are often by definition ambitious and achievement-oriented. As well as hopefully having many ambitions that are for their organization and their team, they will also usually have strong personal goals. Understanding the personal goals and motivators of your boss is part of forming a strong relationship. This is a very individual equation. An easy assumption to make is that senior executives are motivated mainly by financial rewards. However, this is questionable and there is evidence that suggests that financial incentives are at best very limited motivators, particularly in the longer term (Pepper *et al*, 2013). Money is probably important to your boss but it's unlikely to be what drives him or her at a personal level day in and day out.

One generalization that seems to hold up well is that senior people in organizations are often high in need for achievement. This need was recognized in the 1950s by the psychologist David McClelland. It is characterized by a need for achievable challenge. This can mean avoiding both very low risk and very high risk challenges. The former brings no satisfaction because the effort required to attain the goals is insufficient to fuel the need for achievement. The latter carries too many risks of non-achievement, which obviously also fails to satisfy the need. In practice, those with a high need for achievement have a drive to demonstrate, particularly to themselves, that they are advancing and making progress. They also usually require regular feedback to help them evaluate their progress. This doesn't mean you should spend lots of your time telling your boss how fantastic he or she is. Valid and well-delivered negative feedback may be just as important to someone with a high need for achievement as praise and positive reinforcement.

However high your boss's need for achievement, there are probably three key areas where you can serve him or her well in terms of his or her personal needs: being reliable; actively seeking to understand and support his or her priorities; taking a genuine interest in your boss as a person. These themes will be developed in Chapter 7 but it is worth introducing them here in the context of broadly considering what others need from you.

Have you heard someone being called 'a safe pair of hands'? This can be interpreted with a slightly negative connotation: the person is not very dynamic and a bit boring. That is unfortunate because at its core this phrase captures the essence of reliability, which is valued highly by most senior leaders. Building a reputation for delivering what you say you will is the cornerstone of building trust and respect. Senior leaders need to know that those at the next level down in the hierarchy will implement policy and strategy effectively. This reflects on them in terms of their reputation. There is no reason why you can't do this and still be dynamic and influential. There seems to be a personality-based judgement often made in the workplace that you are either reliable and efficient *or* dynamic and exciting. This can and should be challenged. We see no reason why you can't be reliable *and* dynamic.

Understanding the priorities of your senior leader is clearly important in forming a close and effective working relationship. To quote Gabarro and Kotter (2005): 'At a minimum, you need to appreciate your boss's goals and pressures. Without this information, you are flying blind, and problems are inevitable.' This doesn't mean you need to seek to understand everything that your manager is involved in but that you should have real insights into his or her key strategic priorities, and engage in a positive dialogue about these. The relationship here should be one of mutual-dependence. This state is described by Makin *et al* (1989) as like a marriage where both parties understand the needs of the other and agree to regulate their activities to ensure their individual and shared needs are met. This requires maturity and openness on both sides. Arguably you will only be able to support your boss's needs and priorities if he or she also seeks to understand and support yours. However, practically, the emphasis may well be on you to be proactive to ensure this sharing occurs.

Perhaps you should be interested in your boss as a human being, given that most of them are from that species? One of the best indicators of engagement and wellbeing for employees at different levels is the extent to which they believe their manager cares about them as a person. We see no reason why this shouldn't also hold in an upward direction. This isn't necessarily about trying to make your boss your best buddy. It's recognizing that, like you, bosses are complex human beings with a life beyond day-to-day work activities. Occasionally showing a genuine interest in what they do away from work or in their family life is likely to be appreciated. The extent to which you forge a true friendship with them will be determined by a number of factors such as your personality, attitude and interest similarities and differences, and also your respective ages. As experts on generational differences like Erickson (2010) note, younger generations (eg Gen Ys) are likely to feel less concerned about hierarchy in seeking to form friendships. They tend to be less convinced by any attempts to hide behind status or title. Of course where this could get really interesting is when there is a significant age gap between you and your boss.

What do those at lower levels need from you?

Let's switch our perspective to those at lower levels in the hierarchy. To some extent the factors that apply at senior levels hold at lower levels; for example, the interpersonal dynamics in your team will be important. However, our starting point in gaining an insight into the reality of life at lower levels is to draw on wellbeing research. We firmly believe that employee wellbeing is important in many ways. There are clear links between health, productivity and the way people behave in their working environment. Wellbeing has a physical component but it is the psychological aspects that we will concentrate on for now. This is not to ignore the physical side (we revisit this in Chapter 8 in the context of the whole-person approach and lifestyle management), but it is the psychological aspects that are most relevant in terms of day-to-day work experience.

Psychological wellbeing is defined by combining emotional experience and sense of purpose. Experiencing frequent positive emotions at work in tandem with maintaining meaning through staying connected to a purpose you value captures the essence of positive psychological wellbeing. What drives this in the workplace is now becoming well understood. One model that is particularly useful as a lens on the experience of those at junior to mid-levels in organizations is Robertson and Cooper's (2011) ASSET model of workplace wellbeing (see Figure 2.1). Let's illustrate the usefulness of this model by considering how three of the key workplace factors can play out for those at more junior levels: control and autonomy, job security and change, and work relationships.

Figure 2.1 The ASSET model of workplace wellbeing (Robertson and Cooper, 2011)

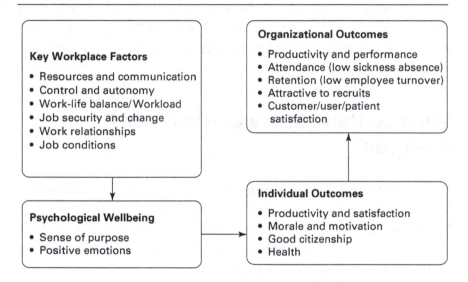

Control and autonomy

Generally, people need to try to take control of their pressures and challenges for the benefit of both their wellbeing and work performance. One result of not doing so is to slip into the learned helplessness state we touched on in Chapter 1. This state is essentially one where you feel powerless to affect your environment. Those that fall into it tend to become cynical and disengaged. Obviously some individuals take more control than others, and personality and prior life experience have a large impact on their tendency to do so. However, those at low to middle levels in organizations often face mixed messages from more senior people on the extent to which they are expected to take control. Take the notion of empowerment. This has been a popular theme for many organizations over the last couple of decades. Many leaders have been encouraged to tell their people they are empowered, to take control and make the right decisions, particularly for those in customer-facing roles. Perhaps you have spent time trying to communicate with your team about the need for them to be more empowered.

Unfortunately, in our experience, the message received by many in lower level roles in organizations is something along the lines of, 'You are empowered but don't get it wrong.' Employees may be asked to take control, make decisions and even take risks to find the right solution. If they do so it inevitably means that they will occasionally make mistakes and get it wrong. But, if they are automatically chastised when this happens, then not surprisingly they won't really believe they are empowered for very long. How managers react when their people make well-intentioned mistakes is very important in determining the extent to which they feel they can take control. It is also influenced by broader factors such as working systems and processes. For example, total quality management-oriented Lean programmes have become popular in recent years in a number of different sectors. In some sectors there is evidence that they can improve employee empowerment, such as in higher education (Barber, 2011), while in others, such as in the international automobile industry (Jones *et al*, 2013), Lean can have a negative impact on empowerment. The reality is that it is leadership and management behaviours that probably have the biggest impact on whether work systems like Lean will ultimately have a positive or negative outcome in terms of empowerment (Poksinska *et al,* 2013). Therefore, it is true that the broader climate and work processes will have an impact on the extent to which people feel empowered and take control, but it is also true to say that the relationship between these is mediated by managers. It ain't just what you do, it's the way that you do it!

Job security and change

Clearly for many people these are uncertain times in businesses and organizations across a wide range of sectors and economies.

Where there are real threats in terms of headcount reductions or redundancies, not surprisingly people will feel more insecure. Middle managers can often be targeted in the first wave of any redundancy programme. However, it is how secure people feel facing change when there is no real immediate threat to their employment status which is revealing. In our experience insecurity becomes problematic when there is a creeping worry that work or the job is changing too radically and people become less confident about either the future direction or their capacity to respond to it. We have all heard the phrase 'change is the only constant' – it has become a cliché. Change is life. However, it seems to be the relentless nature of change that people find difficult to cope with. We also find that it is often uncertainty, rather than change per se, that is the main stressor.

We can all change but clearly vary in how adaptable we are. If you have a team you will no doubt have observed how some people seem more comfortable than others engaging in major change, particularly in its early phases. There are differences based on personality and experience of previous change. Particularly important in terms of the latter is how change in the current organization has been experienced. Those with longer service can easily slip into 'seen it all before' mode. At its worst this can result in a deep cynicism about the organization. Even if it has not created a strong general cynicism, the problem with this attitude is that it predisposes people to adopt an approach that is essentially keeping their head down in the belief that this will all blow over and not really affect them in the longer term. If you are a manager trying to fully engage your people in a change process you will recognize how frustrating and ultimately destructive this can be.

In many ways success in this area is all about building confidence: confidence that change is not only possible but that individuals and teams have the capacity to make it work for them. The last aspect, in individuals, is close to the important idea of self-efficacy. This refers to how effective you believe you are and has been linked to a number of aspects of job performance and wellbeing. Self-efficacy also tends to interact with work pressures to determine the likelihood and severity of stress and level of job satisfaction. This seems to hold up well in different cultures. For example, one study demonstrated how self-efficacy moderates the relationship between work pressures and job satisfaction and stress in Chinese workers (Siu *et al*, 2005). Consider this for people facing new levels of uncertainty in relation to changes in their job. If they are generally confident with a belief in their effectiveness they are much more likely to feel they can cope, and actively seek ways of doing so, than those facing new uncertainty with a starting point of low confidence and self-efficacy.

There are a number of ways of building confidence and self-efficacy in those at more junior organizational levels. We will explore some of these in some depth in Chapter 5 – including introducing a tool for helping you build confidence in your team to meet new challenges. One aspect worth noting here is that some people at junior levels may have concerns that their jobs are not likely to change sufficiently to keep them interested and motivated in the future. It is easy at more senior levels to slip into thinking that because your role may feel like it is constantly changing, this must also be the reality for everyone else in the organization. Some people are at risk of rust out, rather than burn out. Change, even when it appears initially threatening, can ultimately be the driver or catalyst for more interesting and stimulating work.

Work relationships

Relationships are at the core of the quality of most people's experience when working in teams. When relationships are positive, other work pressures seem easier to deal with and wellbeing and performance are enhanced. When they are negative the climate becomes fragile and getting things done seems so much more difficult. At relatively junior levels relationships with peers are important but probably less critical than the line manager relationship. So, if you line manage a number of people, what do they need from you? At the heart of this is how you balance challenge and support. Let's deal with the latter first. It has been shown that the three pillars of how people experience pressure in their working environment, and how they perform, are demands, control and support.

There is clear evidence that people can thrive facing high levels of work demands if they maintain a sense of being able to control what they need to and feel supported (Bakker *et al*, 2010). Feeling supported is more likely if you have key resources readily available that help you to reach your goals, such as the right equipment or accessible technical expertise. However, it is also very much maximized through supportive relationships.

Your people are unlikely to welcome challenge as much as support, particularly immediately. However, they need constructive challenge just as much as they do effective support. The risk of falling into a comfort zone can be quite high for those in junior to mid-level roles in organizations. For those who are generally capable of doing their job, they may after a while start to operate on autopilot. The problem with this is that they can experience negative consequences in terms of boredom and erosion in their motivation. Challenging people isn't just a good idea for performance reasons. When it is done well it is also good for their wellbeing and resilience. You don't build resilience by cruising along in a comfort zone: there is no need to do so. When you challenge someone who works for you it's unlikely that their initial response will be to thank you. That's because their first reaction is often based on the increased strain they are feeling. That's natural, but it doesn't mean they are incapable of rising to the challenge. You are increasing the pressure on your people when you challenge them but this can be positive in the medium and long term.

There is an important distinction between negative hindrance pressures and positive challenge ones. Hindrance pressures are those that you can see no purpose in engaging with other than to get them off your plate. They are perceived only as barriers to success and your initial reaction to them is likely to be 'Why do I have to do this?' Challenge pressures, however, are by definition difficult but they are quickly associated with progress in terms of working towards a goal and/or positive learning. Both types of pressure bring increased strain, although hindrance pressure brings more. Challenge pressures are also associated with increased job satisfaction and organizational commitment, and better job performance (LePine *et al*, 2005). So an important role you can play with your team is to maximize challenge pressures and minimize hindrance ones. We will look at how you can achieve this in Chapter 5.

Understanding the perspectives of those around you

This chapter finishes with a tool that can help you better understand the perspectives of those above and below you in your organization. The emphasis in this is not getting feedback from others: it is in better understanding their needs and expectations. Getting feedback from those at different levels can be valuable, and 360-degree feedback has become quite common in the last couple of decades. However, we believe that it is important to focus first on ensuring you really understand the working experiences of those above and below you before narrowing down to gathering specific feedback on how they see you. The benefits of this should include:

- Better communication between you and those above and below you, enabled by having a clearer understanding of what's important to them.

- Making it easier for you to prioritize your workload because you can better take account of the priorities and needs of others.

- Stronger relationships with more trust and mutual respect. Showing more interest in the needs and working experience of those around you is likely to be appreciated and reciprocated.

The next chapter looks at the pressure you are likely to experience in a mid-level role. Understanding that some pressures are shared with those above and below you and that some are different is a good orientation for considering your own pressures in more depth. The emphasis in the next chapter is very much on what you can practically do to manage the pressures you face well. This will have benefits for you and for those you work with at more senior and junior levels.

PROCESS TOOL

Perspectives: a process to better understand the needs of those at different levels

It is important to understand the perspectives of your colleagues at different levels. It is easy to make assumptions and slip into misunderstandings and conflict when you have a poor or distorted view of how others see your shared experience. This tool is intended to help you develop a more accurate and deeper understanding of the perspectives of those you regularly interact with at different levels. It is intended as a guide to communicating with others to meet these objectives. There are four suggested stages to the process:

1 Capture what you believe others want and need from you.

2 Summarize and rate the evidence you have for these beliefs.

3 Refine and add to the evidence you have, mainly through direct conversations.

4 Restate your beliefs about what they want and need from you.

These stages are explained below and a template is provided for capturing perspectives from more senior and junior levels to the one you populate.

1. Capturing what others want and need from you

There are three aspects to consider here:

a What do they need you to deliver to them?

b What do they want from you in terms of communication (frequency, mode, style)?

c What other support do they need from you?

The first of these is probably the most tangible and easy to identify. What are the deliverables that others need and expect from you? This is usually easier to identify when thinking about your manager or boss than your team or direct reports. However, don't just default to your job description. Consider the key deliverables required currently and perhaps separate short- and longer-term ones.

In terms of communication consider what you think the preferences of others are regarding the way you interact with them and the content and frequency of the dialogue. Remember that communication is not just sending information; you also need to know it has been received and understood as intended. It's worth reflecting on whether you too regularly default to modes of communication that work well for you but are less effective for others (eg overusing e-mail, or regular team briefings).

When thinking through potential support it is useful to consider where you believe others might be stretched. For example, does your boss face a particularly demanding time in terms of strategy review within the next few months? If so, what additional support might he or she really value from you at this time? Remember it is not just about task support; it may be that additional emotional support would be helpful. Perhaps knowing that you empathize with the increased demands your manager faces would have broader benefits for your working relationship.

2. Summarize and rate your evidence

This is about thinking through what real evidence you have for your beliefs. It is very easy to make too many assumptions about what others want and need without much in the way of solid evidence to support our beliefs. In fact the longer you have worked with someone the more likely this is. So when you have captured your main beliefs about what others want and need from you, challenge yourself to identify what these are based on. You may have concrete examples to support your beliefs in the form of conversations you have had directly with the person or people involved. However, it is also possible that you will occasionally find it difficult to justify your beliefs in terms of hard evidence. This doesn't necessarily mean you are wrong but it flags the need to check that your beliefs are valid. You could summarize the main evidence for your beliefs and then rate it using the following simple scale:

1 = I can't really think of any specific or tangible evidence for this belief, it's just my gut feel.

2 = I have some limited specific evidence for this belief.

3 = I have strong evidence for this and can cite a number of examples.

For the beliefs you have rated 1 or 2 you should seek to refine or add to your evidence.

3. Refine and add to your evidence

It is quite likely that you have some beliefs about the expectations of others that have limited evidence but which you still feel are valid. You may be right but you should look to strengthen the evidence that supports such beliefs. Ironically, the best starting point here is to look for evidence that may suggest you are wrong! Confirmation bias is very powerful – having formed a view we tend to pay much more attention to evidence that supports it than to any that appears to contradict it. To avoid this, start by considering whether there is any concrete evidence that would question your belief.

The best way to test the evidence you have for a belief is often to tackle it directly by asking clarifying questions. For example, if you believe that one of your team members is not pulling his or her weight, asking questions such as the following may help: What do you think the team needs from you? How do you see your role in the team? What's your main contribution? In a scenario such as this you may choose to be more direct with less of an open questioning approach. However, such an approach is more likely to get a defensive response and you will usually get less information from the person you are talking to.

4. Restate your beliefs

Having worked through this process you should now restate your beliefs about what others want and need from you. Writing them down will help you to be clear and specific about your beliefs, maybe using a form like the one shown in Table 2.1. You can then decide what action you need to take. This may of course include sharing your beliefs directly with others.

Table 2.1 Perspectives template

What do you believe they want or need from you?	Your evidence for each belief	Refined evidence	Restated belief
List each belief you have	List the evidence you have and rate it using the 1 to 3 rating scale below*	List any additional or counter-evidence you have gathered	Having reviewed the evidence restate your belief

*Evidence rating scale:
1 = I can't really think of any specific or tangible evidence for this belief, it's just my gut feel.
2 = I have some limited specific evidence for this belief.
3 = I have strong evidence for this and can cite a number of examples.

Managing work pressures in the middle 03

In this chapter we explore the work pressures faced in the middle. We start by considering the reality of demand and resource pressures faced in mid-level roles. We then go on to discuss the nature of control from and in the middle. This leads into coping mechanisms with the focus on key areas that are essential for resilience in the middle: a strong social support network, the ability to reframe problems, the importance of core purpose, and accessing resilient role models.

In Chapter 1 we touched on some of the pressures at a general level that those in the middle typically face. Let's develop this further by starting with some insights from monkeys! A recent study found that monkeys in the middle of the social hierarchy in their group suffer the most stress, measured using hormone samples. It was suggested that the results might be generalizable to humans working in middle management positions, to quote the lead researcher Edwards (2013):

People working in middle management might have higher levels of stress hormones compared to their boss at the top or the workers they manage. These ambitious mid-ranking people may want to access the higher-ranking lifestyle which could mean facing more challenges, whilst also having to maintain their authority over lower-ranking workers.

In response to this work, *National Geographic,* somewhat tongue in cheek, suggested four coping strategies that work for the monkeys that middle managers might want to adopt: hanging out with a baby; grooming and scratching; hugging it out; punching something (Poon, 2013). We won't be developing these further in this chapter. We will focus on the main areas of work pressure likely to be experienced in the middle and on the practical strategies that can be adopted to deal with these effectively. Building on the finding noted in the previous chapter that we can deal with high demands when we retain control and feel resourced and supported, we will consider how these three core elements can be influenced.

Demands in the middle

It's the classic pressure sandwich. You get stuck between pressures from above and below, and that's not accounting for those that emerge from your peers at the same level. Of course pressure does not automatically mean suffering negative stress. The stressor-strain model is well established, and holds up well on a global basis (Ralston *et al*, 2010). We are exposed to pressures all the time (stressors) and whether they result in strain depends on our individual reaction.

It is suggested that there are broadly three sources of demand pressure: your working environment, life pressures away from work, and the pressure you put yourself under. Let's consider the last of these first. Your personality and motivation will have a big impact on the level and type of pressure you inflict upon yourself. Of course many of these aspects will be very positive in driving you to success, but strong personality traits and values can be double-edged swords when it comes to stress and strain.

The most robust framework for considering the influence of personality in the workplace is the Big 5 approach (Costa and McCrae, 1992). The Big 5 are: extraversion, neuroticism, openness to experience, agreeableness and conscientiousness. Research often suggests that those that are more extravert and also low on neuroticism are likely to generally have reduced risks of stress-related problems (Kotov *et al*, 2010).

Let's consider one of the other dimensions to illustrate how it can play a role in terms of self-inflicted pressure – conscientiousness. People high on conscientiousness tend to be goal oriented and well organized in their efforts to meet their objectives. Clearly high conscientiousness will be a positive source of drive and motivation most of the time. However, there may be occasions when this causes people to drive themselves unreasonably hard to the point where what they most need is respite. High conscientiousness tends to increase the likelihood of self-directed perfectionism (Stoeber *et al*, 2009). That is the tendency to expect that all you do needs to be perfect. Unfortunately, and I apologize if you are a perfectionist and think this lacks ambition, no one is perfect. Therefore, the risk becomes a combination of driving yourself too hard and regularly beating yourself up because you inevitably fall short of perfection from time to time.

This is a typical example when considering how we can occasionally put ourselves under unreasonable levels of pressure as a result of our personality and motivation. It's a 'too much of a good thing' scenario. To achieve what you have in your life and career some of the attributes that have served you well in striving for your goals can tip over and create problems if not recognized and managed. It's analogous to being over-engaged in what you do. Clearly being fully engaged in your role and your organization is a positive thing and there has been a lot of work in the last decade on improving employee engagement. However, for some, being more engaged isn't the challenge: it's managing the stress risks that come with being over-engaged. The biggest risk associated with this is probably taking on too much and not getting sufficient rest. This can tip you into quite a reactive mode, essentially trying to do more and more without stopping and reflecting on the best way to achieve your goals. In fact, you may even completely lose sight of your most important goals when you get into this state. We need to learn to spot when this is happening and do something that feels completely wrong at that point: *stop*. You may not always spot when you are at the stage where this becomes very important, and that is where colleagues, family and friends are important, if you are ready to listen to them. The most important realization is that this isn't just down to external factors:

you are also causing the way you are behaving and feeling. One approach that is particularly useful in controlling self-inflicted pressures is reframing. We will develop this later in this chapter and illustrate how it can be useful for controlling the pressures we place on ourselves.

Of course not all pressure is self-inflicted. Sometimes life's demands can get excessive. Occasionally this can be completely unforeseen when some sudden or dramatic change occurs; it can also be a creeping build up. We can see and feel it building but somehow convince ourselves that we will just about be able to stay on top of it, until we eventually reach a point where it is clear to us, and probably others, that the demands we face are way beyond our ability to cope. The key here is spotting this trajectory as early as possible and taking action to change it. Easier said than done when you are likely to feel you need every minute just to deal with the demands you face and keep your head above water. So what are the warning signs? Here are some signs and signals that the demands you face are becoming unmanageable. You:

- fill every minute of your diary with planned activity, without any thinking time or space;

- start to do more and more work outside normal business hours;

- have stopped exercising or your level has dropped significantly;

- are more irritable than usual and you stop listening properly to people;

- are not sleeping as well as you normally do; and

- seem to be constantly thinking about what you still need to get done when you are not actually working.

One behaviour that becomes particularly important as demands begin to get unmanageable is saying no. Of course you need to know what to say no to and how to say it effectively. To start with the former, this is all about goal clarity. The goals and objectives of the business or organization need to be clear, as do your team and individual goals. When the organization is not clear on its priorities it becomes very difficult to know what to say no to. We have seen this happen most obviously in recent years in some areas of the public sector, where public and government pressure results in ever-increasing service demands at a time when resources are at best static and at worst diminishing. As one senior police officer said to one of us recently, 'We are frequently told what more is expected of us but never what less.' So in a middle management role the challenge can be seeking clarity from above on the relative importance of key objectives, when those at the top may themselves feel they are struggling to define those priorities. It is always useful to review demands and consider what you should say no to, or at least not at the moment. The old adage that 'A yes is a no to something else' is quite useful to remember.

Saying no well is a real skill, and one that is likely to be important for most people in the middle. For some of us saying no is not what we naturally do. For example, one of the Big 5 personality domains is agreeableness, a large part of which is the desire to please other people. In many ways this is an admirable quality, but people high on agreeableness quite often say yes to requests for assistance without thinking sufficiently about whether they have the resources to really help. It's just their default position to always want to help, and without an awareness of this it can mean saying yes far too frequently. The result will be overload and the added emotional pressure that may result from not feeling great when you let people down.

So what are the key considerations when trying to say no properly? There are probably three main factors: buy yourself time to decide whether you should say yes or no, acknowledge the other person's needs, and stand your ground. When someone approaches you with those dangerous words, 'Have you got five minutes?' you don't really know whether you should have or not. So the first thing you need to do is quickly establish what their need is while at the same time signalling that you don't have time unless what they want is truly important *and* urgent. Saying something like, 'I'm really busy right now but tell me quickly what you need' might work. If they then make you aware of their need you may still not be certain about whether you should drop everything to respond. Two suggestions here: ask whether someone else may be able to help, or say you need to finish something you are working on but will get back to them as soon as you can. Of course if you go for the second option it is really important you do go back to them fairly quickly, even if it's only to say you can't help. Your main goal here is to ensure you don't get dragged into something you don't have time to deal with at that point.

It is useful to acknowledge that you understand that the other person's request is important to them. You can even say you'd like to help but you just don't have time at the moment. It can help to suggest someone else who may be able to provide support, or to say when you may have time to help them if you believe it's important enough to get back to. Finally, you really need to stand your ground quite firmly when you are saying no. That's usually because the other person doesn't want to hear that answer. You may well have to repeat more than once that you can't help them at that stage before they will accept it and look for an alternative. Remember: you are saying no to the task not the person.

Resource pressures in the middle

The most frequently mentioned resource pressure we hear about from those in mid-level positions is the generally perceived need to deliver more with less, or at least more with the same. In the main this manifests as budgetary and human resource pressures. In recent years many Western economies have faced austerity pressures. Some suggest that reduced resource availability can ultimately drive innovation and improvement (Nickerson, 2014; Ward, 2012). Nickerson (2014) also develops an argument that middle managers are particularly well positioned to support innovation and build capability while facing tough resource and broader challenges. There may be longer-term benefits to periods of resource restriction but it will always bring pressures that need to be managed. In the middle you are likely to be involved in budgeting and resource planning but the final decisions on level of resource may reside above you. When resources are more limited than they have been in the past you need an engaged team prepared to co-create new solutions to demand problems.

The first requirement in dealing effectively with resource pressures, particularly with your team, is acceptance. You or your team members may not like or agree with the resource limitations faced, but if this is the new reality acceptance is crucial if you are going to make progress. It is easy for teams to get stuck in denial mode. This can result in constantly complaining about a lack of resource or talking frequently about how much better things were in the past. This can become self-fulfilling in that the perception of inadequate resources results in the team failing to make effective use of the resources that are still available to them. We are not arguing for passivity: it is perfectly possible to continue to argue for more resources while accepting the level of current availability and getting on to utilize what is there to best effect.

Assuming you can move your team into an acceptance mode, what is the next step in dealing with significant new resource pressures? Essentially the key requirement is to review your main objectives and how resources are currently allocated to them. This can serve two useful functions. The first is to ensure you have shared clarity concerning your main objectives and priorities and the second is to potentially identify how progress can be made by reducing or reallocating resources between priorities. Doing this frequently is important. Just doing it at set points, such as when preparing an annual budget, is usually insufficient. Building resource reviews into regular team interactions can help to add to a sense that you are doing all you can to actively and optimally allocate resources.

It is also important to remember that we are not only concerned with tangible resources here, like budget or staffing numbers. Support in less tangible forms is an important part of the equation. This might be in the form of useful guidance and coaching. If you receive this regularly you will appreciate its value. In many ways one consequence of this is helping individuals to maintain a sense of control when facing excessive demands and resource pressures.

Control in the middle

In Chapter 1 we painted alternative pictures of life under pressure in mid-level roles. In the positive version we suggested that the middle might be the best place to be when it comes to exerting control. There is a logic to this in that from the middle you should have more points of contact and visibility across the organizational span of control than those in higher or lower positions. However, whether you feel a sense of control, and subsequently exert sufficient control, probably rests on two prerequisites: your level of engagement and your ability to exercise control effectively.

In 2010 The Boston Consulting group published global data suggesting that engagement levels had fallen furthest for middle managers through the financial crisis triggered three years previously (Caye *et al*, 2010). They contrasted this with top level managers and lower level team members. Their solution was that a new DEAL was required for middle managers, using this acronym to signal:

De-layer the organization and create larger exciting roles for middle managers.

Empower managers to act.

Accelerate leadership skills.

Leverage the power of middle managers.

These are all positive suggestions, but of course they bring challenge pressures with them. Let's just consider the last of these; leveraging the power of middle managers. We drew on Pfeffer's (1992) definition of power in the last chapter with its emphasis on influencing behaviour and changing the course of events. Influencing behaviour requires more than the use of formal processes and mechanisms such as performance management and rewards. These are important, but it is just as much the informal day-to-day interactions that influence behaviour. A strong starting point in seeking to do this is your own behaviour.

We will develop our ideas on influencing in different directions in later chapters but the start is to take a proactive approach to influencing others to control work pressures. Two key areas to focus on here are content and style. Let's begin by thinking about content in respect to influencing upwards, and to some extent sideways with your peers. There is very little to be gained from preparing and presenting a long speech to your boss or peers about how you are under too much pressure. This is mainly because their first thought will frequently be along the lines of, 'We are all under pressure, you just need to deal with it.' Obviously some of your colleagues will be more sensitive and naturally supportive than others, so you won't always get this reaction. However, it's a weak basis for canvassing support. A stronger approach will be based on seeking a shared view of the pressure faced, combined with an explicit results orientation. Start by asking questions about how the other person is currently experiencing demand or resource pressures. You will be much more effective in gaining support by generating a shared problem-solving mode than by just trying to recruit support to solve your own problems.

The style of communication you use with colleagues at the same and more senior levels is important. Increasingly a consideration in global organizations is the impact of cross-cultural differences on communication style (Smith, 2011). If you report to a boss with a very different cultural background, this is something you should actively seek to understand. There appear to be particular differences based on how individualistic or collective the individual's cultural background is (Hofstede, 2001). Those with an individualistic cultural background, typical in Western democracies, will tend to place an emphasis on having the freedom to pursue individual needs. Therefore, when facing high levels of demand or limited resource pressure, their response is likely to be rooted in seeking to understand how they can improve their own position and alleviate the pressure they feel as an individual. Those from a collectivist culture tend to place the emphasis on the needs of the group; this is more typical in many Asian cultures. So if you are from the United States and work for a Chinese boss you would be well advised to consider how you can present your concerns in a way that places a heavy emphasis on the needs and achievement of the team.

In Chapter 2 we discussed the need to understand the strategic needs and drivers of those at the top in the organization. This provides a clue to where mid-level managers have most scope to take control. When there is strategically-driven change there is a greater opportunity for those in the middle to take more control. The main reason for this is that senior managers are likely to recognize that to successfully implement strategic change they need middle managers to get fully on board and take control. It is also a time when demand

and resource pressures are likely to be heightened. In an interesting qualitative study, Mantere (2008) argues for eight enabling conditions for middle managers taking more control when facing strategic change. These include tangible process factors such as resource allocation, but also less tangible ones such as respect and trust. This highlights the fact that you are only likely to be able to take and exert sufficient control in the middle when you have firm relationship foundations, particularly with those at more senior levels.

One area where we find mid-level people in organizations have particular pressure issues is in handling electronic communication. While this is relevant in terms of demands and resources, it seems to have a particularly strong impact on managers' sense of control. E-mail has been the most obvious example in the last quarter of a century. It is a mode of communication that was rapidly adopted, to the point that for many people in the middle it now seems to dominate their working life. In many ways this seems to be a mixed blessing in terms of control. On the one hand e-mail, and other forms of electronic communication, allows us to stay in touch whenever and wherever we choose to, which should enhance your sense of control. On the other hand, the sheer volume of e-mail, particularly for middle managers, can leave you feeling swamped with an increasingly diminishing sense of control. In an excellent paper on the stress associated with e-mail, Barley *et al* (2011) identify a number of key issues in the relationship between e-mail and stress levels. One factor they identify is the importance of expectations regarding response to e-mail; they exemplify this by quoting a marketing manager:

> I'm very good about responding to e-mail. I rarely let things sit without a response for more than a day. I'll respond saying either I've done it or that I'll look into it or whatever. Even if I have not completed an action, I'll let them know that I'm working on it. So because of my personal thing, I expect people to respond to me within a day or so when I send them e-mail. (Barley *et al,* 2011: 899)

In our experience, managers often make all sorts of assumptions about e-mail response expectations with very few attempts to share or discuss these explicitly with their colleagues. As a result, they can create confusion and misunderstandings that can result in relationship and efficiency problems. Nevertheless, it is certainly true that many mid-level employees are overloaded in terms of the sheer volume of e-mails they receive.

There are some strategies that appear to help in trying to maintain control when facing this. One is to be disciplined about when you access your e-mail. Just responding to each e-mail as it drops into your in-box may make you feel you are avoiding a backlog and boost your immediate sense of control. However, the risk is that you get drawn into reactively responding to a fairly random set of priorities. This can mean that the short-term satisfaction gained from maintaining your in-box without a backlog is at the expense of dealing with what is truly most important. You may gain the immediate gratification of feeling you are controlling an important workload pressure but ultimately feel less in control as you are not being proactive enough in focusing on what is most important in the longer term. The suggested solution isn't to allow your e-mail to pile up excessively but to choose times when you tackle it. Perhaps you schedule three time slots in your working day to access your e-mail and try to stick to those. One additional advantage of this approach is that you can quickly scan the e-mails that have arrived while you have been offline and decide how best to distribute your time between them. If you have been used to responding as e-mails arrive you will probably find this approach very difficult to stick to. You have to fight the feeling of not being in the loop in the gaps between your chosen response times. You may have to disable e-mail alerts on your phone or other devices to prevent you immediately responding. Try it for a month and see what impact it has on your overall sense of control and ultimately your performance and wellbeing.

Whether you adopt this strategy or not it's important to recognize where you have choices when it comes to dealing with e-mail and indeed other sources of potential overload. Your personality plays a role in the choices you make as does the working climate you are immersed in. Generally, we all need to use effective coping mechanisms to deal with demand and resource pressure and maintain a healthy level of perceived control. We go on now to develop some that have a positive impact for many who utilize them.

Pressure in the middle: coping mechanisms

Ensuring you use strong, active pressure coping mechanisms is critical for your wellbeing, performance and development. The remainder of this chapter will outline key coping approaches that are tried and tested, and particularly relevant to those occupying mid-level positions. The overall concept we will use to structure this part of the book is psychological resilience, which we introduced in Chapter 1. We made reference to Charney's work on resilience and the four factors he and his colleagues emphasize that we will develop here in relation to managing pressure in the middle:

1 Establish and nurture a supportive social network.

2 Develop cognitive flexibility – ability to reframe stressful events.

3 Develop a personal 'moral compass' or shatterproof set of beliefs.

4 Find a resilient role model (Southwick and Charney, 2012).

1. Supportive social network

We vary in terms of how much social support we need, influenced by our personality (Bowling *et al*, 2005), but we all need some. You may generally be a self-sufficient person when it comes to handling pressure; however, it is a mistake to slip into believing social support at work is not that important for you. This belief increases the risk of becoming isolated and turning round one day when you need support and finding that none is readily accessible. As demands increase we are much more likely to maintain our wellbeing and engagement if we retain control and feel we can actively draw on social support. An interesting research project across eight European countries confirmed this and found that while perceptions about demands and autonomy/control varied significantly across countries, social support was more consistent, with only the Swedish feeling they had significantly higher levels of support (Taipale *et al*, 2011). Interestingly, Sweden is often held up as an exemplar of a psychologically healthy, socially supportive Western European society.

As noted above it is easy to get isolated in the middle if you seldom pay attention to your social support network. A key question to ask yourself is: 'Who can I have a safe conversation with?' A safe conversation is one where you believe you can share problems or issues with another person without worrying about negative consequences in doing so. If you have someone you trust to respect confidentiality, unless you divulge something illegal or unethical, this can serve as a useful pressure buffer. It is likely to be sustained when both parties value the capacity to have the safe conversation, and both invest in maintaining the relationship.

A supportive social network need not be restricted to work colleagues. In fact, for many people family and friends away from work are likely to be their main source of social support. However, there are risks if you believe you have no social support at work. On many occasions the support of family and friends will be useful and adequate but there are some issues where support from colleagues who understand the context is likely to be more useful. Of course having a supportive boss is particularly beneficial.

A useful reflection activity here is to list the people in your life you rely on for social support. Include anyone you might only interact with occasionally if you still believe the relationship provides you with useful support from time to time. Perhaps capture them on a blank sheet of paper with you in the middle. Consider the size and shape of your support network; some key questions to ponder are:

- What does the balance look like in terms of colleagues at work in comparison to friends and family away from work? Are you over-reliant on the latter?

- Do you think this has changed significantly in the last year or two? If it has, do you think your support network is stronger or weaker than it has been in the past?

- Is there anyone in your network with whom you need to work to strengthen your relationship? Is there a risk of losing their support through neglect?

There is no universally right or wrong social support network. However, there will be an optimal network for you in terms of the amount and range of support you have available. It is something we can easily neglect in dealing with the day-to-day activity that work and life throw our way. Stepping back occasionally to review and strengthen your support network is likely to be a good investment.

2. Develop cognitive flexibility – learn to reframe

Figure 3.1 Stressor-strain model and how we frame our reality

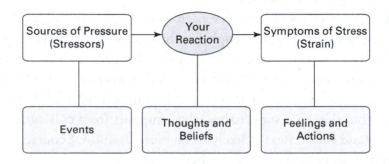

Figure 3.1 relates the stressor-strain model to the influences that frame our reality at an individual level:

- *Events:* stuff happens (sometimes expressed more negatively!) Can we control what happens to us? Sometimes, but often we can't. If you are feeling stressed and can influence events, this may well be the place to focus your attention. It is always worth considering whether you have more influence over events than initially appears to be the case. However, if you have limited or no control over what's happening then you need to concentrate on how you are reacting.

- *Thoughts and beliefs:* there is not a direct line between events and how we feel and what we do. Events are filtered by our thoughts and beliefs about what is happening, and it is the combination of these that determines our feelings and actions. We tend to develop thinking habits that we apply, usually unconsciously, when something happens to enable us to quickly make sense of it. Sometimes these can be helpful shortcuts that help us make good decisions, but some thought patterns can be less helpful and serve to amplify our stress levels, and leave us uncertain about the right course of action.

● *Feelings and actions:* understanding that our feelings are the result of events plus thoughts and beliefs begins to open up the possibility of exerting more control than we may previously have thought we had. When we react to increases in demand pressures by taking particular actions, such as working excessive hours, it's important to recognize this is a choice rather than being absolutely determined by what has been happening in our environment.

The reframing process is primarily based on the well-established cognitive behavioural approach. This has grown from a range of psychological theories and therapeutic models over the last half a century or so. In the form of CBT (cognitive behavioural therapy) it has become one of the most frequently accessed psychological therapies for those struggling with anxiety-related problems. We are not going to attempt any therapy here but will demonstrate how a form of the approach can be helpful in coping with the pressures faced in the middle.

Let's work this through using an example. Imagine (or recall) a situation where your boss has asked you to undertake a challenging piece of work in an unrealistically short timescale. She apologizes to an extent when she presents this and acknowledges that she recognizes the difficulty of what's being asked of you. However, she also makes it quite clear how disappointed she would be if you didn't accept the challenge and deliver what's required. Your initial feelings might be anxiety, irritation, but perhaps also a sense of pride? What thoughts or beliefs might drive these emotions?

Often the most difficult thing to do is to recognize and capture the thoughts that are driving your feelings. By their nature they are fleeting and we are seldom fully conscious of them. It takes time to reflect on what lies between the events or situation and our emotional response.

Clearly some of the thoughts shown in Table 3.1 are unhelpful, both in terms of the associated emotion and trying to identify the best course of action. One way of understanding these thoughts is to draw

Table 3.1 Common emotional responses and linked thoughts/beliefs

Emotional response	Thought or belief
Anxiety	'There is no way I can achieve this in the expected timescale, there just aren't enough hours in the day.'
	'I'm going to have to drop everything to achieve this, which means I'll get way behind with my other work.'
	'This means I'm going to have to work late every night. I'll have no time for my family and I'll be exhausted by the end of the week.'
Irritation	'This is totally unfair; I should have been given much more time to deliver this.'
	'My boss is always doing this, failing to give me enough notice because she can't plan and organize properly.'
Pride	'She must really trust me and my team to ask me to deliver this important challenge.'
	'My boss knows this is a stretch but she must have a lot of confidence in me to ask me to take this on.'

on what we know about how people tend to attribute the cause of events. Attribution theory is useful in trying to ensure our thoughts are constructive rather than destructive. This has its origins in the work of social psychologist Bernard Weiner (1985). Two key aspects of how we attribute causality to what has happened are whether we think in terms of external or internal reasons, and how stable the causes are likely to be over time. Let's take one of the thoughts from the above example to illustrate this: 'My boss is always doing this, failing to give me enough notice because she can't plan and organize properly.' This is an example of an external and time-stable attribution. It's 'my boss' not me who is doing this (external) and she is 'always doing this' rather than it being a one-off or infrequent occurrence (time stable). The resultant emotional response is irritation, so how valid and helpful is this thought? The core of the reframing process is to capture and challenge our core thoughts and beliefs. The fact that cause here is external may have some validity but there may also be internal reasons for the situation occurring. For example, perhaps you could have been more proactive in staying closer to the priorities of your boss and strategic changes? The time-stable attribution here is definitely worth a challenge. Does your boss really always do this? Probably not. It's much more likely that because it has happened more than once it is being overgeneralized to 'always'.

Classically when something isn't going well and you are feeling lousy and uncertain about your best course of action the attributions that are most helpful are external and temporary. So, using the above example, an alternative thought could be: 'It's impossible to predict all urgent workload increases, they happen from time to time.' This would fit the bill. However, there is probably a case for a long-term helpful approach being a mix of attributional types, particularly in terms of whether they are internal or external. Constantly believing that nothing is your fault probably isn't realistic or helpful in the long term. In fact, it could be a contributor to learned helplessness where you believe you have little power to influence events. It's probably more useful to hold beliefs that are a mix of internal and external attributions. The optimal balance is not to beat yourself up forever when something goes wrong that you have a responsibility for, and not to dismiss all problems as being caused by others or external events.

In a mid-level position, reframing can be very useful for maintaining your own resilience but also for understanding and challenging how those above, below and around you are framing their reality. Perhaps you could apply this to someone who reports to you. If you believe that one of your team members is not helping him or herself by interpreting an event in a particularly negative way, using a reframing conversational structure can be very useful. You do this by working through five key stages:

1 *Situation* – ask the person to tell you what has actually happened. This can be more difficult that it appears to be as he or she is likely to have raced way beyond this in terms of thoughts and feelings.

2 *Feelings* – how does he or she feel about what's happened: angry; embarrassed; anxious; let down?

3 *Thoughts and beliefs* – this is where you really need to listen carefully to what is being said. Try simple questions like, 'What is making you feel so angry about what has happened?' or 'Why do you feel so let down by this situation?' There will probably be a few core thoughts and beliefs that sit between what has happened and his or her feelings.

4 *Challenge and consider alternatives* – not all thoughts and beliefs are due to negative faulty attributions; some are rational and evidence-based. The key here is to challenge the core thoughts and beliefs (revealed at the previous stage) to encourage the person holding them to consider whether they are based on real evidence. Some will be and it's then a case of exploring how to deal with the likely consequences. In the example above the anxiety-provoking thought that a task can't be achieved in the available timescale may be supported by evidence that other similar work has taken much longer. Therefore, the appropriate action may be to seek to renegotiate the timescale, supporting the argument with evidence from previous experience. However, if on reflection there is evidence that other equally challenging tasks have been successfully completed in similar timescales then it's worth questioning the belief. It is also important to consider any reasonable alternatives at this stage. When we experience negative or stressful emotions it is likely that we get too narrow in our perspective. Some people are aware of this to some extent when they feel stressed and they find it difficult to concentrate on anything other than the main thoughts that are anxiety provoking. In Chapter 1 we mentioned the 'broaden and build' theory of positive emotions; the opposite when stressed may be the 'narrow and destroy' impact of negative emotions. At this stage in the conversation it is worth asking the other person whether, having talked through the issue, he or she can see any alternative way of thinking about it. Often he or she will think of something relevant. You may also have thought of something he or she hasn't mentioned that you think is a potentially valid way of conceptualizing the problem; if so, suggest it here. It is important not to offer what you believe is the right way to think about it or a solution too early in the conversation. From your position it may well be the case that you have a perspective on the issue that the other person doesn't but offering it too early destroys the reframing process. The purpose of this conversation is to first and foremost understand how the other person is framing the issue and to help him or her reflect on this and realize that there may be other ways of framing it. It is not to get him or her to adopt your framing of the issue. If you want to cut to the chase and be directive about a solution then do so, but recognize that this is direction, not reframing.

5 *Most appropriate actions* – finally, ask the person what he or she thinks the best course of action is. Occasionally this will be quite a radical repositioning and a new line of intended behaviour. It may be a more subtle change of intention, but this in itself can be useful. If there is not an immediate change of intent the conversation may still play an important role in helping the other person understand that, with a bit more reflection, there may be alternatives.

This isn't counselling or psychoanalysis. It is a straightforward structure than can be applied in a 15- or 20-minute conversation to good effect.

3. Develop a core purpose or moral compass

We have already mentioned that sense of purpose is a defining component of psychological wellbeing. At a deeper level, having a strongly developed core purpose or moral compass can serve as an important source of resilience. This will be particularly important when facing a crisis in your life, personal or professional. In our experience, when people meet a major crisis they need to draw deeply from within themselves to rebuild. This may be an illness, bereavement, break-up of a close relationship, redundancy, or any other major life-changing experience. However, perhaps it's a high risk strategy to wait for a crisis before you work out who you are and what really matters to you. Having a well-developed sense of this acts as an anchor that keeps you rooted through all of life's experiences. Powerful questions are important here; for example:

- What do I believe in that I am unwilling to compromise on?
- What do I most want to contribute to the world?
- What brings me most fulfilment and joy in my life?

Questions like these are not meant to be easy to answer. They are intended to get you to think deeply about who you are and what your deepest values and beliefs are. Examining your core purpose or personal moral compass can be uncomfortable, particularly if you come to the conclusion that they are somewhat distant from the values and culture of your organization. If this is the case, it's arguably better to realize this sooner rather than later. Staying for a long time in an organization that does not fit with your core belief system is likely to result in a growing disaffection and possibly decreasing self-respect.

One goal of this book is to suggest that middle managers would benefit from finding more positive core purpose in middle management activity. We mentioned in Chapter 1 that the image of the middle manager has been negative for some time, perhaps almost to the point of demonizing the role. However, there are voices that speak for a different frame of reference:

> As a group, middle managers are central, indeed crucial, to an organization's success... Middle managers should be valued for what they contribute and be seen as a resource to be developed. Such a perspective is more accurate, healthier, as well as one that would be more productive for all concerned. (Osterman, 2009)

Based on his research, Osterman describes middle managers as craft workers. This is an interesting perspective. The opportunity to be a craftsman or woman, and the intrinsic motivation that crafting something can bring, is perhaps more obtainable now in middle management than in other roles in most organizations. Skilled hands in manual crafting are disappearing as technological manufacturing becomes ever more automated. The crafting of an organization's outputs is perhaps mostly achieved with the ingredients that middle managers have most access to. As Osterman (2009) puts it, there are:

> four characteristics of craft work: the work is intrinsically interesting, employees have an opportunity to use existing skills and learn new ones, the work is an end as well as a means, and employees believe that their work is an important component of their personal identity.

Obviously this is a positive view of middle management in terms of both opportunity and attitude. However, we believe it is obtainable and lived by many. Craft pride, through the creative and effective exercising of middle management activity, can be a strong intrinsic motivator that becomes part of your core purpose and identity.

Having a strong core purpose or personal moral compass provides a stable base for resilience in facing many challenges. However, there may be some risks in terms of inflexibility, or even a lack of respect for those with other beliefs, particularly in relation to moral compass. These are worth monitoring and mitigating through tolerance and the recognition that others may also hold strong core values or beliefs that are different to ours. At a collective level, in teams and organizations, there is power in diversity of thought and belief. You may have a very strong sense of who you are and what matters to you but so may others and they are often going to be different. Wouldn't it be a frightening, or at least less interesting, world if we all had the same core beliefs?

4. Find resilient role models

Think of two people in your life who you think are resilient and one other who is the least resilient person you know. Do the two resilient people have anything in common that differentiates them from the least resilient person? We have asked this question of many people in resilience training and coaching sessions. The format, based on Kelly's (1963) personal construct theory, is designed to get at what people identify as resilient qualities and attributes. This is the basis of understanding who people identify as their resilient role models.

The usefulness of this is that it serves to remind us that we can learn from others in terms of coping with pressure and resilience. In mid-level roles it is probably helpful to have more than one resilient role model; perhaps one at the same level as you and one at a more senior level would be helpful. You are going to get most from identifying resilient role models if you can interact with them to discover more about how they deal with pressure. Of course what they do to deal with pressure may or may not work for you in the same way, but developing an understanding of how others you admire deal with pressure can provide a fresh perspective and impetus to change what you do for the better. You may also discover that while you have identified someone as resilient, this doesn't necessarily match how they frequently feel. Some successful people learn how to portray an image of being calm and in control that might be very different to how they feel.

You may also find inspiration in the apparent resilience of those in the public eye who seem to overcome adversity and succeed in facing major challenges. A few years ago at Robertson Cooper we ran a fun poll asking people in the UK to rate a range of well-known public figures in terms of their resilience (Robertson Cooper, 2010). These ranged from Nelson Mandela to the UK model and celebrity Katie Price. Perhaps not surprisingly Mandela was rated as the most resilient by a substantial margin. In second place was the, now discredited, cyclist Lance Armstrong (a good warning about the risks of hero worship). The most interesting aspect of this was the findings on what people saw as the key source of resilience: overwhelmingly, it was sense of purpose. This was true in all cases, with the exception of how respondents viewed Katie Price: they thought her main source of resilience was self-confidence rather than purposefulness. Perhaps when we can't see a clear purpose in others we assume they must have other qualities that drive their resilience, so when we look at famous people as resilient role models it is probably their mission and purpose we seek to understand for inspiration.

The last point to make about resilient role models is to keep in mind that *you* may be someone else's role model, particularly for members of your team and less experienced managers or leaders. This may not be something you welcome but it's analogous to leadership generally: if you are followed you are a leader, whether you choose to be or not. Therefore, the way you deal with pressure and your behaviour generally may be seen by some as something they seek to learn from or even replicate. We will develop this idea further in terms of the pressure climate you create for your team in Chapter 5.

There are other factors outside of work that add to the pressures we face and how we cope with them; we will consider these in Chapter 8. At work, in the middle, it boils down to understanding that negative reactions to pressure are caused by the interaction between the external pressures you face and your state, traits and belief systems. There will be times when you can exert significant control on the external pressures faced and this can be the right choice. However, there will also be many occasions when this is limited or non-existent. It then comes down to understanding and influencing your response to those pressures, and the response of those around you.

There is a direct link between the work pressures you face and your performance, motivation and development. We do not see these as areas to necessarily consider separately: they are interdependent. In particular, we have spent a lot of time over the years trying to convince managers and organizations that wellbeing and performance go hand in hand. Of course you can perform at a high level for intense periods and your subjective wellbeing may not be great, but you can't sustain it unless you look after your wellbeing in the long term. There are also links between managing pressure and motivation and development. The next chapter will explore how you can stay motivated and keep developing your career in mid-level positions. Development takes place in a pressure context. While pressure can be stressful it can also be the source of motivation and a spur for development.

Mid-level career development 04

In this chapter we examine career development in mid-level positions. The middle is where many will spend most of their career and it is important that they continue to develop in this space. We begin by discussing career anchors in this context. We then examine the importance of looking out and across from a mid-level position, connecting through effective networking, and creating multiple options when planning career direction. The chapter includes a template for capturing and structuring your career development activity. It concludes by highlighting the important considerations for those responsible for supporting mid-level career development.

So where are you in your career? If you sit mid-level in a large organization you already have a track record of success. You can build on that, but the starting point is deciding what you want to build. At the end of Chapter 1 we asked you to consider your career development goals and provided a number of prompt questions to help you to do this. If you tried to answer these, have a look back at what your responses were. In many ways these prompts were trying to get you to consider your core purpose relating to your career. We talked about the importance of core purpose in the last chapter in the context of maintaining wellbeing and resilience: having clarity about your career goals and purpose can produce a dual win in terms of your development and long-term wellbeing.

Career anchors

One approach that has been widely applied and used over the last quarter of a century is Schein's (1990) career anchors. These are values-based preferences focusing on what is relatively most important to you in terms of your career. Schein describes eight anchors:

1 Technical/Functional competence (TF) – you value your technical or functional competence highly, you are happiest when you stay close to this and are less likely to enjoy general management activity that takes you too far away from your technical or functional expertise.

2 General Managerial competence (GM) – you value being a generalist rather than a specialist, suggesting you will be happier in a broad role where you do not have to apply specific specialist skills too frequently and can focus on general performance and the integration of activity.

3 Autonomy/Independence (AU) – you highly value the freedom to define your own work in your own way. You will tend to be least happy when you feel too tightly constrained by your organization in terms of what you can do and how you do it.

4 Security/Stability (SE) – you value stability and security (financial, employment tenure). We all have some need for security (and indeed autonomy) but being anchored by this means you need to feel *very* secure about your future.

5 Entrepreneurial Creativity (EC) – it is important to you to be able to create something new; building your own business strongly appeals to you.

6 Service/Dedication to a cause (SV) – you value serving humanity, a cause that is important to you or bigger than yourself.

7 Pure Challenge (CH) – you value difficult tough challenges for their own sake, tending to seek novelty, variety and having to reach for the near-impossible.

8 Lifestyle (LS) – you value a balanced lifestyle and flexibility, with work as part of your life rather than all of it. Family and friends away from work carry a high priority for you.

These career anchors appear to work well cross-culturally and have been applied and researched in countries such as South Africa (Coetzee and Schreuder, 2011), Taiwan (Chang *et al*, 2012), Malaysia (Rasdi *et al*, 2009) and Canada (Quebec) (Wils *et al*, 2010). They have also been used in the context of global working and expatriate adjustment (Cerdin and Pargneux, 2010). Schein tended to argue for a dominant career anchor but others have questioned this, suggesting multiple anchors are more likely for many people.

Keeping in mind that career anchors are just one lens on career development, they provide a starting point for considering development in mid-level roles. It is useful to understand the anchors that are most important to you. On the face of it some anchors seem more congruent to a career in a hierarchical large organization than others. For example, valuing general managerial competence (GM) is likely to make you more comfortable as you progress to middle management-dominated levels. In contrast those who value entrepreneurial creativity (EC) may get increasingly frustrated if their role in the middle brings more and more bureaucracy and the need to operate within tightly defined processes. However, many large organizations in recent years have recognized the need to create the space and freedom to encourage entrepreneurial creativity within their architecture; this is sometimes referred to as 'intrapreneurship'. This has been shown to have a number of different dimensions that could be routes those with an EC career anchor may find it stimulating to pursue. To illustrate this let's take three dimensions from a deconstruction of intrapreneurship proposed by Antoncic and Hisrich (2001), which they developed using samples drawn from Slovenia and the United States:

1 *Product/service innovation* – if you can find a mid-level role where you are responsible for continually improving and innovating the product and/or service offering of your business this may be very satisfying and serve your EC need.

2 *New business venturing* – if you are in a sales or marketing role you may meet your EC need by being able to open up new lines of business and extending the proposition of your business in new and different ways. Another form of this is related to organizational

structure where you form new business units that can operate semi-autonomously from the host organization. The rationale here is to exploit potential new opportunities without being tethered to an existing culture that would probably be too slow to adapt to take advantage of the situation.

3 *Self-renewal* – where the self is primarily the organization, but perhaps this also works at the individual level. This is where the entrepreneurial instinct can be harnessed to creatively renew and reinvent the business or organization through strategic change and reshaping.

It is almost certainly true that some career anchors will fit better with some organizations than others. If your values suggest career anchors that do not traditionally fit well within large and complex structures, and you are within one, you are likely to need to work harder to find a development path that works for you. For example, if you have life-style (LS) as a strong career anchor you may find that, in middle to senior level roles, finding the time and space to focus on relationships and activities away from work becomes increasingly difficult. If you have dependants and value your time caring for and nurturing them, you may find a level of understanding and flexibility from your employer. But what if your lifestyle drive is to spend a significant proportion of your time on non-work-related hobbies and interests? How would your boss react if you asked for flexible working to allow you to get more surf time in at the beach or write your novel when you felt most inspired? It would take a particularly liberal employer to accommodate such requests regularly, although perhaps doing so would make good business sense.

There is some evidence that enlightened employers are beginning to consider the benefits of accommodating personal interests and life-styles beyond the workplace. For example, for many years Google has allowed its employees to spend 20 per cent of work time on projects driven by personal interests; a policy that was subsequently adopted by other Silicon Valley companies. There are some mixed reports about whether this freedom remains in place at Google as it originally operated. There is also a growing dialogue regarding the benefits of mid-career sabbaticals (Allen *et al,* 2011). However, this is often from the perspective of advocating a regenerative break rather than a long-term lifestyle-oriented shift.

In many ways, all of the career anchors pose challenges and there could be points in your development when there is a conflict or misfit between your values in these terms and where you are with your organization. For example, if security/stability (SE) is an important anchor for you and your company is taken over, or there is a prolonged period of uncertainty regarding future size and shape, you are likely to get more uncomfortable than many of your peers. Depending on the strength and nature of your SE anchor it may be that even changes affecting your role that carry no real threat to your employment status feel very difficult and provoke significant anxiety. If you can see that the role demands you will face in the future appear very different to those you have honed your skills from in the past, you may feel less secure. Essentially the key to not allowing a strong SE preference to become a frequent source of stress in an increasingly changing world is to find a foundation you can feel secure about when you meet periods of increased uncertainty. This could mean building your confidence that you have the ability to adapt to change and that you can, and almost certainly have, developed your skill base to meet new challenges. Thus, your need for security is served by feeling more secure in your own ability to change and adapt successfully. This anchor may also be partially served by having a stable family life and non-work-related activities that you value and can rely on.

The technical/functional competence (TF) career anchor is particularly interesting at the mid-level career stage. Valuing this, particularly related to technical competence, is likely to serve you well when your career stage is essentially pure specialist. However, at mid-levels your role is likely to be primarily leader of experts rather than expert. We frequently meet specialists promoted into middle management roles who find the transition extremely difficult. Successfully managing this transition usually means that to some extent you need to stop doing what you are really good at and has been reinforced positively to this point. If you are a technical specialist, say an engineer or a scientist, with a strong TF anchor, directly applying your specialist expertise much less than you have done in the past is unlikely to be easy. Working through this probably means finding a way to satisfy the TF anchor through enabling technical or functional excellence from your team or those who report to you. This essentially means being able to let go and transform the way you operate by:

- *Accepting* that you cannot continue to apply your technical/functional competence as directly as you have done in the past; that you need to become less hands on.

- *Releasing control* of activity that used to be totally within your control.

- *Developing* a new way of leading that provides meaning that satisfies your need for technical/functional involvement and excellence.

This is easier said than done in many cases. The most difficult stage is often the first. When you are immersed in technical or functional expertise and becoming an expert in your field has been the key to your career success so far, accepting that you need to let go of some of this is very difficult for many. To do so you need to truly believe that to be effective going forward you will need to operate differently. Perhaps one way of enabling this is to adopt the crafting purpose referred to towards the end of the last chapter. If you believe that through middle management activities you can play a key crafting role in working with others to build better technical solutions, this may well serve your TF anchor drive. You may even begin to see how you can play an enhanced role in achieving technical excellence through effective middle management within your field. In practice many managers acknowledge this as the rational, logical change but still find the behavioural change required beyond them.

Behavioural change pivots around the second stage: releasing control. Being ready to release control is not just about accepting it is necessary to allow you to be more effective: it also means accepting that those you release it to will probably be less capable than you and will make mistakes. The emphasis shifts to enabling the technical or functional excellence of others rather than just delivering your own. Crucially at this stage you need to allow others to make mistakes and your reaction when they do so is important in determining whether you will be able to make a successful transition. If you jump on them when they get it wrong and immediately criticize, they are likely to start to play it safe and avoid taking control if they perceive the task as risky in terms of success likelihood. We will expand on this in the next chapter in the context of getting the best out of your team.

Ultimately, this transition is about developing a new way of working that allows you to lead experts well while retaining your TF anchor. This requires finding meaning through facilitating the technical or functional expertise of others to thrive, and see and feel that you play a major role in this. It is also finding a way to retain your TF application and satisfaction without constant hands-on implementation. As noted above you may see that you can craft technical excellence through middle management. In addition, an option that many organizations now support is to develop 'guru' status. Many technical and scientific organizations now have dual career paths: a technical/specialist path and a managerial path. This makes sense in that it allows those who want to stay close to their specialist expertise rather than generalize into management to advance and gain increased responsibility and reward. However, it is not a given that this route will be the best one to take in the long term, even if you have a strong TF anchor. It is possible that the technical guru route could ultimately feel too narrow and constraining, even if your specialism is very important to you. Perhaps it is worth at least exploring the appeal of a broader managerial role while staying close to your area of technical/functional expertise before taking the narrower path.

What if your strongest career anchor by some way is autonomy/independence (AU)? In many ways this is likely to serve you well in middle management. It suggests you will naturally be driven to take control and make things happen. However, there are obvious risks in terms of not consulting sufficiently with others, particularly your boss. This is worth bearing in mind as you read Chapter 7, which focuses on managing upwards. If you need to be autonomous and independent to flourish you will have to be open about this and negotiate what that means in practice with your manager. Of course how you express this might be very relationship-oriented in which case the potential risks in this career anchor might be mitigated. For example, you may be working on a project that requires little input from others and you can take largely independent decisions to successfully progress it. If you keep others informed regularly regarding your progress and invite their thoughts they are unlikely to believe you are not involving them sufficiently.

The service/dedication to a cause (SV) anchor is an interesting one for a middle manager. At a number of points throughout this book we suggest that having a well-developed sense of purpose is advantageous. If your purpose is serving others or to a broad cause then this is likely to be particularly beneficial for your wellbeing. It reduces the risks of becoming too inwardly focused and slipping into a victim mindset. It is clearly an anchor that is tied to deeper values. One tool that you may find useful if your career anchors and choices are firmly tied to deeper values is the Life Values Inventory developed by Crace and Brown (1996). This is useful regardless of your specific preferred career anchors, particularly in the context of taking a whole-person orientation (which we argue further for in Chapter 8) to career choices. However, it will probably resonate most with those who have a strong SV anchor. For example, it includes scales such as 'concern for the environment', 'concern for others', 'humility' and 'spirituality'. In practice, finding a service orientation or deeper cause that fits with your organization's values and ethos is likely to be very important to you if SV is a core career anchor.

You may place a lot of emphasis on being exposed to tough challenges with pure challenge (CH) as an important career anchor for you. This will have many benefits in that you will look for stretch and this builds capability and resilience. It can also mean not necessarily being most motivated by hierarchical position or financial rewards which, if your career is to continue positively at mid-levels, is probably advantageous. You will tend to find periods when you are not particularly stretched difficult and disconcerting. However, on balance this seems a positive driver for those seeking to manage their career laterally and looking for new challenges in different areas and activities across the organization.

Looking out and across

You may be driven to reach the top in your business or organization, in which case defining goals that are likely to lead to further promotion and plotting potential routes to the top may well be the best tack for you to take. However, as formal organizational hierarchies flatten, the opportunities at the top are becoming fewer and more competitively sought. Interestingly, the drive behind flattening or de-layering organizations has usually been to increase empowerment at the front line but in some cases may have had the opposite effect of further concentrating control at the top (Wulf, 2012). The reality for many is that reaching the top is either an unlikely or unattractive option, or a combination of both. If this is true for you, your focus should be on how you can develop your career effectively in a way that brings you continued fulfilment in mid-level roles. There are three broad areas that we will now focus on that should help you to do just that:

1 *Looking out and across* – you need to be able to effectively scan your career environment for future opportunities.

2 *Connecting* – networking within your organization and beyond is increasingly important for creating new development opportunities.

3 *Creating lateral futures* – it is very unlikely that your optimal career development path will be linear and predictable, so opening up and exploring multiple potential paths is usually a good strategy.

It is very easy when you are in a busy middle management role, and probably a hectic life beyond work, to narrow your perspective to the immediate. Continuing to develop your career means occasionally stepping back from your current demands and reality to attend to what is happening more broadly. It is literally lifting your head. Given that it is inevitable that the majority of your time and focus will be on immediate demands it becomes ever more critical to actively create the time and space to look beyond what is right in front of you.

Fostering a curiosity about other parts of your organization and people beyond your regular circle of contacts is a strong starting point. If you work in a large business or organization, how well do you know what happens in other divisions or departments? When was the last time you had a non-task-related conversation with someone beyond your regular direct contacts about what they do? This is the kind of activity that we usually tell ourselves we don't have time for. However, it is becoming clear that there are some very real learning and cognitive benefits to being curious about other people and activity. Research demonstrates that a curious state helps you learn better about the target area you want to know more about (Gruber *et al,* 2014), which is not surprising. So if you are genuinely curious about what one of your peers does in a different functional area you will learn more about what they really do than if you were tasked with doing so as a matter of routine. However, a particularly revealing additional benefit is that you are likely to remember more of what was generally happening around you when in a curious state. Given that what you may learn helps your career development is incidental to what you intended to learn, this is an important finding.

Gruber and his colleagues (2014) also found that curiosity brings its own rewards. To quote one of the researchers behind this work discussing what happens in the curious brain: 'Curiosity recruits the reward system, and interactions between the reward system and the hippocampus seem to put the brain in a state in which you are more likely to learn and retain information, even if that information is not of particular interest or importance' (Ranganath, quoted in *Psychology Today,* 2014).

Developing your career without a hierarchical promotion will be considerably enabled by a curious mind that looks outwards and beyond daily boundaries. The activity that this drives can become motivating in its own right, and therefore intrinsic and self-sustaining. Becoming more curious about your organization and the people within it can give rise to habitual exploration, which will generate its own rewards and increases your chances of serendipitous development. However, it needs to be accompanied by more goal-directed strategies in two main areas: connecting through effective networking and scenario planning future options.

Connecting through networking

Networking: a word that drives fear into the heart of many introverts! That's usually because we have a stereotypical view of what networking means, such as working a room and swapping as many business cards as possible. This is a narrow and outdated view of networking in the modern world. However, just as there is more to networking than 'pressing the flesh' there is also more to it than complete reliance on social networking tools such as LinkedIn. Julia Hobsbawm, a professor of networking in the UK, provides an interesting take on networking that is relevant to mid-level career development: 'Networking has to happen at a personal level and it has to spread laterally across organizations, building knowledge flows, sharing information, and building confidence and connections' (Hobsbawm, 2014).

When you think about it, being in the middle in a large organization is the optimal position for effective networking. You should have multiple points of contact upwards, downwards and sideways. The key is probably truly valuing networking for its own sake rather than necessarily as a short-term means to an end. In some ways this brings us back to the nature of power in organizations. Hobsbawm's networking definition places an emphasis on open and shared knowledge flows. To engage as a willing and active participant in this you need to accept that power is not dependent on clinging onto your own knowledge security blanket. It's not knowing lots of stuff that is a strong basis for advancement but knowing how to apply what you know in new and innovative ways. Content knowledge has never been more accessible, but its useful integration and process innovation are less easy to find and replicate. Through open and frequent networking across and beyond your organization you can enhance your potential to find new innovation pathways. This broadens your scope to develop your career. Ironically, the way to compete in terms of mid-level career development may be to more fully cooperate. Not surprisingly those wedded to a more traditional hierarchical development model will find this counter-intuitive and uncomfortable.

Putting career development to one side there are also strong reasons for thinking that improving your networking skills will be generally useful to survive and thrive in the changing context of many organizations, particularly in the middle. There are growing arguments that effective organizations need to become powerful networks to meet the challenges of future change in the wider business, political, social and technological environments in which they function. Satell (2015) provides a useful overview of some of the considerations and issues and argues that 'organizations actively discourage connectivity. They favour strict operational alignment within specific functional areas while doing little to foster links between them'. If this feels true of your organization, it suggests that networking will not be enabled by the structures and processes you operate within. However, if there is a trend towards networked organizations then adopting an active networking approach may position you well as change occurs. In fact, it could become a key differentiator for future progression.

Reviewing the research on career networking it is very apparent that much of this still focuses on networking as a tactic for hierarchical advancement. It could simply be that there is a lag between real-world relevance and published organizational research or, more worryingly, it could represent a real collective mental barrier to moving away from this paradigm. In our view effective networking is a key enabler of development, but not necessarily hierarchical promotion.

One aspect of Hobsbawm's definition that is particularly important in the context of lateral career development is building confidence. Having the confidence to network without imposing unnecessary limits or boundaries around yourself will take time to build for most people. The further you move out of your immediate circle of contacts and connections the more fragile your networking confidence is likely to become. This will hold most strongly when reaching out to those that you perceive to be higher status individuals. It is important to remember that networking is not selling. In connecting with another person because you believe there may be mutual advantage in doing so, you are not asking them to buy anything. In fact, if you are trying to sell them something then it's better to be open about your motives and not confuse by conceptualizing or presenting what you are doing as networking. There is nothing wrong with selling, but it's a different activity.

The other advantage to networking is that it will be good for your wellbeing. In Chapter 3 we discussed the important of building a supportive social network, and we will revisit this theme later in the book. Here we place the emphasis on networking as a career development strategy but a by-product of doing so is quite likely to be a strengthened supportive network. Two birds, one stone.

Creating lateral futures

The idea of a single narrow path you plan your career progression around may still work for some but it seems increasingly difficult, and risky. Difficult because of the unpredictable nature of organizations, career opportunities and individual goals. The last of these should not be underestimated. Your career goals may well change significantly as you go through life. For example, you may value a different work-life balance as your family responsibilities increase, or you may get excited about a radical change in career direction. It also seems increasingly high risk to plan for a predictable linear, narrow career journey.

A strategic analogy that is useful here is the idea of a value chimera. A chimera in Greek mythology is a multi-headed beast with a single body. In borrowing this as an analogy for strategy development, Cummings and Angwin (2004: 28) note: 'The chimera gains its strength by having many formidable and flexible heads or faces which it can present to confront distinct challenges, while efficiently operating these heads from one solid but agile platform.'

Now we are assuming you literally only have one head, but staying agile in career terms might mean that you need to virtually develop a number of different ones. The starting point is being clear about the core body you are working from. This is where clarity about your core purpose, career anchors and values is critical. From there, what might your multiple heads look like? Some suggestions for the heads you may grow are your:

- Within-function head – how can you develop within your existing functional area? For example, do you need to update your functional or specialist skills?
- Broad organization head – looking beyond your function, department or division to what other roles you might be able to play in other parts of your organization.
- Competitor head – how aware are you of what competitor organizations and businesses are doing in terms of their shape, direction and the roles available within them?

- Life tangent head – what other interests do you have in your life that could open up a whole new career direction? What do your friends do that might complement what you do and could lead to new collaboration?

Of course creating a career chimera will be enabled by curiosity and networking. However, it also means making the time and space to create your chimera and review it. Whether this analogy works for you or not, the principle of actively considering alternative career development paths is sound.

Career resilience

We discussed resilience in the last chapter and will revisit it later in the book in the context of life pressures beyond work. A number of researchers and practitioners are interested in resilience related to career transitions and trajectory. When applied this often seems difficult to distinguish from general resilience development, just placed within a career context. For example, Beverley Jones, a coach, in an interview by Hannon (2012) offers six key steps to career resilience:

1 Get connected.
2 Choose optimism.
3 Learn something new.
4 Think like an entrepreneur.
5 Look at the big picture.
6 Get in shape.

Of these probably only one of the steps, 'think like an entrepreneur', is specifically career-related. However, Jones makes a very telling point: 'Even if you feel like a cog in the middle of a big organization, you can run your career like a one-person business.' This is a positive and active way to think about career development in the middle and fits with an emphasis often made in this area about the need for career self-reliance.

This idea also includes thinking about your personal brand. One of the largest global management consultancies, PWC, provides a useful open access online workbook for developing your personal brand (http://www.pwc.com/us/en/careers/campus/assets/img/programs/personal-brand-workbook.pdf). Interestingly the content of this has a clear cross-over with the key aspects often highlighted to enhance psychological wellbeing and resilience, the four main themes of the PWC resource being: Soar with your strengths; Tap into your values; Pursue your passions; Define your purpose. Essentially resilience is important for health and wellbeing as well as career development and there is evidence that targeted interventions can simultaneously make a difference on both fronts (Vuori *et al*, 2012).

A key aspect of career resilience is understanding and developing your strengths. A strength is something you naturally do well, enjoy doing, and tend to find energizing. Of course we all have weaknesses and it's important to recognize yours in relation to your career development and ambitions. Ignoring your weaknesses is likely to derail you sooner or later. However, focusing only on developing your weaknesses is a recipe for a distinctly average outcome. For career development it is particularly useful to identify and develop latent or underused strengths. For example, perhaps you are a very capable negotiator and have enjoyed doing so to reach a successful conclusion in the past, but your current role provides few opportunities to use this strength. How could you open up possible avenues to use this strength more frequently? Perhaps your boss would welcome an offer of help to support negotiations with suppliers or agents?

Broadly three areas go a long way in starting to structure your thinking about strengths in a work context:

1 *Problem solving and decision making:* perhaps you are very analytical or comfortable making quick decisions with only limited information, or you could be good at opening up alternative solutions that others don't easily see.

2 *Interpersonal strengths:* what do you do well and enjoy when interacting with others? Perhaps you are good at building new relationships. Is your strength being a very active listener and helping others clarify their thinking? Are you good at defusing tension in emotionally charged situations?

3 *Staying motivated:* what drives you and keeps you going when it's tough? For example, do you have a strong purposefulness built on being clear about your values? Alternatively, you may feel you are at your best facing particularly tough circumstances and that you raise your game when this happens.

While this is a good starting point if you are serious about understanding your career strengths, you should use a strengths based diagnostic. For example, in the United Kingdom, Capp's R2 Strengths Profiler is an increasingly popular tool (http://www.cappeu.com/R2StrengthsProfiler). It measures no fewer than 60 attributes based on performance, energy and use. It specifically highlights unrealized (latent) strengths as being important for career development. In the United States, The Via Institute has developed a profile that rank-orders 24 character strengths into six broad areas: wisdom, courage, humanity, justice, temperance and transcendence (http://www.viacharacter.org/www/Character-Strengths#nav). Tools like these can help you think about the breadth of strengths you may have and identify them with a high degree of specificity. This helps when trying to put together a development plan using your strengths. It's worth bearing in mind that it is possible to overuse strengths. This tends to be less of a risk with latent strengths you are seeking to further develop than it is for well-developed signature strengths.

Career resilience is also about having strong adaptive coping mechanisms in place particularly when you face major transition or uncertainty. Generally, it's useful to have some flexibility about the coping mechanisms you can draw on. You may have a strong rational coping approach enabling you to easily and logically think through how you are framing an issue. This is likely to be very helpful but it may be a mistake to over-rely on it and underutilize other proven coping techniques such as drawing on social support.

Wellbeing and career development

As we have already noted, doing the right things to continually develop your career in the middle is very likely to also enhance your wellbeing. The two are interdependent to a significant degree. Based on an analysis of extensive global survey data, Rath and Harter (2014) highlight five core elements of wellbeing and argue that the most important one in terms of its overall impact is career wellbeing; albeit they define this very narrowly as whether you like what you do every day. Burn-out is a risk that needs to be managed as your career progresses and changes, but so is rust-out. The latter refers to the risk of becoming progressively disengaged, demotivated and frankly bored. The consequences of psychological burn-out are usually painful and dramatic, with health implications, but rust-out can creep in slowly and less visibly, particularly in the early stages. It is avoided by actively ensuring you stay connected to activity that has meaning for you. There may be a period in your career when rust-out is a greater risk for you than burn-out. You may tolerate the former for longer than the latter but the results of not recognizing and addressing it will be negative for your career and your long-term wellbeing.

The strongest link between wellbeing and career development is probably meaning and purpose. If you are in a mid-level position in a large organization it should be possible to experience a meaningful career without promotion to the most senior level. Of course it would be naive to think that all organizations are equally supportive of this and there is little doubt that career resilience requires a large degree of self-reliant development.

PROCESS TOOL

Structuring your career development

Figure 4.1 illustrates how you can continually develop your career in the middle. There is an upward dependency in the key activities necessary to successfully develop your career in middle management roles. Understanding your career anchors provides a strong foundation and starting point. Whatever you do from there, it's going to require resilience. Looking out and across and connecting through networking are essentially interdependent and probably most effective when executed simultaneously. Finally, all of the above feeds your capacity to successfully create powerful lateral futures.

Tables 4.1 to 4.4 are intended to support you through this career development process. While there is a hierarchy of sorts to the areas, you shouldn't feel too

(Continues on p 81)

Figure 4.1 Bringing it all together: structuring your career development in the middle

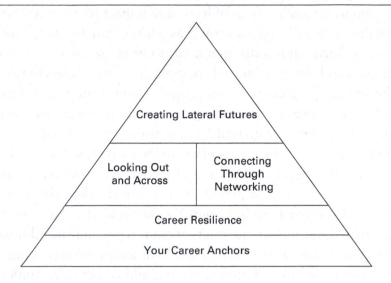

Table 4.1 Your career anchors

Prompt questions	Your response
How do you see yourself in terms of your interest in remaining close to your specialist expertise in comparison to becoming more of a managerial generalist?	
What's the optimal balance for you between freedom and independence on the one hand and security on the other?	
Are you driven by the need to create something new and prepared to take significant risks to make it happen?	
How important is service to you? Do you gain your greatest satisfaction from serving and enabling others? Do you live for a specific cause?	
Do you need tough, perhaps even extreme, challenges to really motivate you?	
Do you live to work or work to live?	
Complete this sentence: 'What matters most to me in my career is…'.	

NOTE: There are questionnaires available that can help you specifically identify your career anchors and understand their comparative importance. Schein's Career Anchors Self-assessment can be purchased from a number of sources including Amazon.com.

Table 4.2   Boosting your career resilience

Activity	Your experience in this area
Exercise: How habitually do you exercise? How does your psychological state vary when you exercise regularly in comparison to when you don't?	
Bouncing back: What has been your largest career setback so far? What did you do to recover from this?	
What would you do similarly and differently if you meet another major setback?	
Playing to your strengths: List what you believe your strengths are, starting with three broad areas: 1. problem solving and decision making; 2. interpersonal/interacting with others; 3. staying motivated.	
How could you use these strengths more frequently or in different ways?	
Avoiding burn-out: What strategies do you use to:	
– Ensure you don't continuously work hours that are excessive and potentially damaging to your health and family life?	
– Prioritize well to ensure you deal with what is truly most important and regularly make time for your own development?	
Avoiding rust-out: What strategies do you use to:	
– Recognize when you are stagnating or stuck in a rut and need to do something different to stay motivated?	
– Ensure you occasionally do something well outside your comfort zone?	

Table 4.3 Looking out and across and connecting through networking

Activity	Frequency and effectiveness
Exploring an area of your organization or business that is fairly distant from your function/business unit.	
Actively seeking to build relationships with your peers across organizational or functional boundaries.	
Expanding your network beyond your organization or business.	
Attending networking events such as conferences.	
Going beyond just inviting people to connect on social networks such as *LinkedIn* by exchanging ideas or information with them.	

Table 4.4 Creating lateral futures

Sketch two, maybe three, alternative career paths you believe are possible and motivating. Describe what success would look like along these paths at three different time points (eg in two years from now, five years, and 10 years).

You could do this as a Fishbone or Ishikawa diagram if you are familiar with that approach, or in any format that makes sense to you.

Career Path 1.

Career Path 2.

Career Path 3.

bound by that. You may feel that one area needs more attention than others or choose to focus on 'higher level' activities even when you know you have considerable work to do at lower levels. Don't be a slave to the process here: adapt and use it as you find it to be most helpful.

Supporting others to develop their career in the middle

If you are responsible for the development of middle managers there are a number of considerations worth building into your strategy and plans. We highlight three we believe should be prominent in your thinking:

1 Middle levels are full of talent that is at risk of being underexploited.

2 Developing people in the middle may be the most cost-effective way of developing the whole organization.

3 Engagement across the organization should improve as the mid-level population develops.

In the last two decades, talent management has come to the fore as one of the most dominant HR paradigms. This appears to have been kick-started by McKinsey's work in the 1990s presented in *The War for Talent* (Michaels *et al*, 2001). In the early years the talent movement tended to place all the emphasis on the very top performers – those considered destined for the top. However, this was gradually challenged and a broader, less elitist, approach to talent management emerged. For example, the leading management consultancy KPMG recently highlighted three key approaches companies are now taking to talent management that fit well with the ethos of this book:

1 Enlist and empower management in talent management – don't just leave it to HR.

2 Focus on developing clear career paths.

3 Take a holistic approach to talent management across the entire employee population. (KPMG, 2014)

The middle levels in your organization or business are full of talented people. However, there are risks that they feel undervalued and that not enough emphasis is given to developing and releasing their full potential.

If you want to maximize your bang for your buck in terms of management development spend, then the middle is the obvious place to concentrate on. A successful programme here resulting in behavioural change will have an impact from the middle upwards, downwards and sideways. In particular, this can have an impact on employee engagement across the organization. In fact, this is something that we would encourage you to measure as an outcome from significant development programmes targeted at mid-level employees.

To increase the likelihood of achieving long-term benefits from mid-level development programmes we would encourage you to adopt peer mentoring and/or action learning approaches to embed the development. Peer mentoring can be very powerful: for example, it can facilitate increased knowledge creation and sharing (Bryant, 2005). It supports networking across organizational boundaries and encourages participants to take ownership of their longer-term learning and development.

Career development: the need to influence outwards

We have argued in this chapter that, if you are in a mid-level role, you need to create time and space to properly focus on yourself. However, this doesn't mean becoming self-obsessed! Hopefully, through adopting our emphasis on areas such as looking outwards and networking, this risk is reduced. Nevertheless, the day-to-day influence you have on those around you is important for short-term performance and wellbeing reasons, but also facilitates your longer-term development.

We develop not just through deliberate attempts to do so. We learn and grow through our everyday relationships with others. The next three chapters focus in depth on relationships with your team, your peers and your boss. Our working relationships play a central role in our wellbeing, performance and long-term development. Of course our relationships away from work are also important and we consider these in the context of broader life management in Chapter 8.

Getting the best 05 out of your team

In this chapter we focus on getting the best out of your team. We start by reinforcing the basic elements of effective teamworking, which are often not as strongly in place as they need to be to provide the platform for team effectiveness. We heavily emphasize the importance of team resilience and wellbeing, arguing that these are inextricably linked with team performance and can be managed holistically. Within this we place an emphasis on key factors such as balancing challenge and support, and ensuring we make the most of positive experiences and play to strengths. We discuss the importance of properly understanding and managing the team's pressure climate. The need to see your role leading and managing your team as a core part of what you do, and being able to let go sufficiently to allow the team to succeed and fail, are also underlined. At the end of the chapter we provide a short but powerful guidance tool for building and maintaining team confidence – something that we believe often fails to receive the attention it deserves and needs.

Do you enjoy leading and managing a team? This can be the most fulfilling activity that you engage in as a middle manager. It can also be among the most demanding and frustrating. In this chapter we will provide useful insights and techniques for getting the most out of your team. As well as ensuring your team perform consistently well for their sake and the benefit of your organization, the aim is to enable you to get the most from your role as a team manager and leader. We will also work from the basis that getting the best from your team can be done in a way that maximizes their wellbeing and performance. In fact, we argue that high levels of team performance are much more sustainable when wellbeing levels are also high.

Teams – getting the basics right

We still find that teams often fail to get the basic principles of effective teamworking right. There are three core tenants we focus on: shared goals, autonomy and interdependence.

Shared goals

Teams often assume they have shared goals but may not be sufficiently explicit about what they are, or they fail to review them regularly enough. These should be well defined, and what success will look and feel like when you attain them should be shared. The emotional part of this is important. Having a rational description of what goal attainment will mean is useful but on its own can be a bit dry and not very energizing. For example, a manufacturing business team may have as a goal: 'To produce consistently high quality goods with a defect rate of <1 per cent.' This may be enough to consistently motivate some but you would have to agree it's a bit bland at best. It's not necessarily about replacing this goal statement with something more deliberately inspirational like: 'To amaze and wow our customers with the high quality of our goods which never fail to deliver what's promised.' Stating goals in this manner is fine if they are truly more motivational to those who have to deliver them, but language that is over-flowery and looks like it has been devised by a brand marketing team can backfire. It also tends to get less specific and introduce more scope for interpretation. The key is sharing the expected emotional response to goal attainment. So based on the previous example how would the team feel if they frequently met their goal. Proud to be associated with such high quality? Content, based on believing your efforts have resulted in tangible highly valued outcomes? Sharing these feelings within the team when they occur and discussing their anticipation can play an important part in sustaining shared goals.

Ideally shared goals will be sufficiently stretching to be motivating but not so ambitious that they are considered completely unachievable. There is nothing wrong with having a range of goals some of which are more stretching than others. Some teams we have worked with talk about beer goals and champagne goals (although alcohol does not need to be the currency you adopt!). The important point is that they are properly shared. As well as sharing in terms of understanding there also needs to be true shared emotional commitment; the latter can fail to receive sufficient attention. Assuming a shared level of commitment is dangerous. However, discussions about this aspect need to be open and authentic. Just asking, 'Are we all on board then?' and watching nodding heads is rarely sufficient. If there are objections to, or uncertainties about, team goals they need to be aired. As a team leader your role here is to ensure you have a process in place that not only allows these to surface but at times actually encourages them to do so. This is likely to include some one-to-one conversations as well as team-based discussions.

Autonomy

Teams need a level of autonomy. Autonomy enhances the team's working knowledge, skills and ability that members bring (Leach *et al*, 2005). To reach their potential teams need to understand where they have control and autonomy and also the limits to this. Too little autonomy, perceived or real, will prevent the team reaching its potential. The distinction between perceived and real limitations is not always easy to draw. Ultimately if the majority of the team believe they are limited in some way then they are: perceptions are reality, but they can be changed. For example, a sales team may believe they don't have the remit to significantly change the customer offer or proposition. However, a useful initial test of this is to challenge them to recount examples of where they have tried to do so. There is a high risk of self-limiting beliefs developing in teams, particularly those that have been stable in their composition over a significant period of time. The language used in teams sometimes makes this apparent. When you frequently hear about what 'they' would like or allow, it can be time to challenge assumptions, starting with who 'they' are, and then asking for evidence to support beliefs about how much autonomy the team is perceived to have or not have. Once again this is another illustration of learned helplessness.

Team autonomy is an important dimension in team performance but also has implications for the wellbeing of team members. For example, Van Mierlo and colleagues (Van Mierlo *et al*, 2007) showed that team autonomy predicts team wellbeing when the former was experienced in the day-to-day work activities that team members engaged in. This is an important point: the general condition of the team in terms of their goals and autonomy levels will only really have a full impact if they are woven into the work team members regularly undertake. The fact that autonomy can improve wellbeing and performance is a dual win and one that can form a virtuous spiral. For example, as team performance improves team members will feel good about it and probably strengthen their purpose: key aspects of wellbeing. As a result, they are likely to make the most of the autonomy they have and perhaps seek to push boundaries and take more control.

Interdependence

Interdependence is probably the most important and least well understood determinant of effective teamworking. This relates to working on problems that can only be solved by team members working together to do so. Many problems can be solved without the need for teams. In fact, using teams to address some problems is wasteful and inefficient. Serial problems that can be broken down into discrete linear component parts are better addressed by individuals working independently and then collating their efforts. Teams should spend most of their time on complex 'wicked' problems that can only be solved through frequent interaction between team members. Defaulting to teamworking for many straightforward problems is inefficient. It results in process loss: the process of trying to interact to solve the problem actually detracts from the capability to solve it efficiently. If you lead a team you need to decide which problems need you to truly collaborate to solve them, requiring interdependent working. The kinds of thinking prompts that can help here are:

- Can I easily break this problem down into discrete parts or is too much of it intertwined and difficult to decompose?
- Do I need my team members to exchange ideas and debate them to move this forward?
- Does it look like I need team members with different expertise and experience to work together closely to make progress here?

Team resilience and wellbeing

Resilience

A core message of this book is that wellbeing is fundamentally important for a wide range of reasons including work performance and productivity. This is true at different levels: for individuals, teams and whole organizations. We have already discussed the importance of psychological resilience, but here we want to focus on this as a characteristic of teams rather than individuals. The same core definitions apply but we will now concentrate on how well equipped teams are to maintain their collective performance under high levels of pressure, and how well they bounce back from setbacks as a team. When your team is facing a particularly tough challenge, what reactions do you see? Do they seem to bind together to meet the challenge or does it mainly open up divisions and result in dysfunctional behaviours? Team resilience is essentially about what happens interpersonally whereas at an individual level it is mainly intrapersonal. In teams it's mainly what happens between individuals rather than within them that determines resilience.

One relevant concept here is Bandura's (2000) notion of collective efficacy. This is a development of individual self-efficacy but with the focus on how effective team members believe they are as a team. Bandura, reviewing the research evidence here, concludes that: 'the higher the perceived collective efficacy, the higher the group's motivational investment in their undertakings, the stronger their staying power in the face of impediments and setbacks, and the greater their perform-ance accomplishments' (2000: 78). This strongly suggests that trying to get a handle on your team's collective efficacy is important, as is trying to exert influence to maintain or improve it.

Two main interpersonal aspects worth considering in this context are the roles that people play under pressure and how well team members challenge and support each other. It is important to recognize that there are different forms of challenge and support. In the work we have done with Robertson Cooper we have frequently used a tool that looks at the nature of challenge and support based on personality: Leadership impact (Flint-Taylor and Robertson, 2007). Although this was originally designed to help better understand individual leadership style in a traditional line managerial relationship, it provides insights that are useful within teams. This tool highlights two types of challenge and two types of support:

1 Challenge orientation
   - Pace: challenge to operate at high energy levels and flexibly respond to a wide range of different tasks.
   - Results: challenge to stay focused on main goals in an organized and disciplined way.

2 Support orientation
   - Cooperation: supporting collaborative working and open sharing, working to ensure everyone is happy with decisions and that there is strong trust between team members.
   - Confidence: supporting colleagues by building their self-belief and confidence in what can be achieved individually and collectively.

All four of the above approaches are positive, and are all needed at different points in the lifecycle of a team. However, issues tend to emerge when one or two of the approaches dominate and there is a lack of flexibility in adopting the most appropriate mode to suit the demands of the situation: essentially, you can have too much of a good thing. Table 5.1. illustrates key risks to team functioning if a single approach dominates to the point where others are not appropriately used.

Table 5.1 Too much of a good thing

Too much PACE	Too much COOPERATION
Team members chaotically dashing around in different directions, responding on the basis of immediacy rather than real importance/urgency.	Spending too long consulting each other to ensure everyone is happy about everything. Possibly getting overloaded frequently due to slow decision making.
Too much RESULTS	**Too much CONFIDENCE**
Narrowly focused team lacking the flexibility to respond as demands change to the point where there is a need for a real change in direction or strategy.	Team believes it is indestructible and that members can achieve anything to the point where they don't assess risks properly and disregard important warnings.

As well as risks in overusing particular approaches there are also risks in underutilizing them. For example, insufficient results focus can lead to being too easily distracted from the most important objectives or not being sufficiently planned and organized to achieve them. Team members will have individual preferences, based on their personality, but teams need to balance their adoption of different modes and identify when one is more appropriate than the other.

One approach that often seems to be taken is to strive for a perfectly balanced team in terms of behavioural preferences. A team roles perspective, particularly based on the work of Belbin (2010) is frequently applied as part of an attempt to find the ideal balance within a team. However, seeking a perfectly balanced team in terms of the personalities and preferred roles of its members may be a holy grail that is unlikely to be achieved very often. There is great merit in seeking to build teams that have a diversity of approach but, in practice, particularly in a mid-level role, you may have limited scope to select team members to achieve the perfect mix. Therefore, rather than focus on personality, it is often more useful to concentrate on process. To take an example based on the above framework, if you can identify that you do not have a team with many people who naturally work cooperatively, what processes can you put in place to ensure cooperation when required? Table 5.2 shows examples of the kinds of process that may help when there appears to be a deficit in terms of particular approaches based on the leadership impact model.

Table 5.2 Compensating for not enough of a good thing

To compensate for insufficient PACE	To compensate for insufficient COOPERATION
• Review key projects to identify where a new approach or ideas may be necessary to unlock inertia. • Challenge the team to bring you one new idea per month for a new product or service innovation.	• Challenge the team to collaborate to produce an improvement in the way they work together every quarter. Include this as a standing item for review in team meetings. • Create 'open mic' type sessions where a team member can bring a problem he or she is struggling with to the team and ask for ideas and input. • Encourage cross-boundary working by inviting each team member to form a new relationship with someone in a different part of the organization and bring their learning back to the team.
To compensate for insufficient RESULTS	**To compensate for insufficient CONFIDENCE**
• Regularly review progress against plans and objectives. • Insist on good meeting discipline with clear agendas and starting and finishing on time. • Encourage regular sharing of a small number of team key performance indicators with metrics in place to monitor them.	• Encourage the team to share their collective strengths and achievements at least once a quarter (consider doing this monthly). • Ensure you regularly express your own confidence in individuals and the team collectively. Why do you believe they can achieve more than they already have?

Confidence

It's worth focusing on one particular aspect of the framework: team confidence. Looking at the kinds of activities and processes that support the above areas we have often found that building team confidence is the poor relation. Just thinking about typical operational and business processes illustrates why this might be the case. We are likely to focus on the delivery of results and in creating the pace, energy and flexibility required to be innovative and solve problems as they emerge. From time to time we are also likely to concentrate on ensuring people within the team and beyond it are cooperating and collaborating to achieve business goals. However, how often do we take a step back and consider the confidence levels in our team? It is easy to see how this will be a much less frequent orientation. In our work in recent years with Robertson Cooper we have also found that confidence, assessed with the Leadership impact tool, is the weakest of the four approaches in terms of default leadership style.

Building team confidence is the kind of 'sharpen the saw' activity that Covey (1992) discusses and highlights as being so important for long-term effectiveness. It can occur naturally through a combination of success and having a good level of optimism in team member personalities. But confidence is fragile and can be eroded relatively quickly facing setbacks.

Building confidence is in part about ensuring that there is a healthy ratio of positive to negative emotional experiences. Barbara Fredrickson, whose 'broaden and build' theory we introduced in Chapter 1, argues that there is an optimal positivity ratio of 3:1 (Fredrickson, 2009); that is, regularly experiencing three positive emotions for each negative one. While Fredrickson concentrates mostly on individual emotional experience, Losada and Heaphy (2004) show how this holds with teams. A key role you can play from a middle position is to try to influence this positivity ratio in a number of directions. We will come back to how this can be exerted upwards and sideways in later chapters but let's start by considering how you can achieve this with your team, and in doing so help bolster their long-term confidence.

First of all, it is important to recognize that we can often discount positive emotional experience in favour of the often more powerful negative experiences. We often ask middle managers whether they feel like they obtain a 3:1 positive:negative experience ratio and they frequently say it feels like it's the other way round! Perhaps for some it is, but we often challenge this on the basis of the relative power of emotional experiences. In the course of a busy working week you probably have many pleasant and positive conversations, interactions and experiences. However, if you have just one strong negative experience it can change your perception of the overall emotional tone of the whole week. Negative emotional experiences are usually much more powerful than positive ones. This is a key reason why we have occasionally to explicitly work to share and make the most of positive emotional experiences, particularly in a team context. As the work of Fredrickson and her colleagues shows, our emotional experience is banked. The benefit of regularly achieving a 3:1 positivity ratio is that the positive emotional currency more than counters the negative capital and we achieve a net benefit. The exact ratio may turn out not to be exactly 3:1, but as a guiding principle it has real practical value.

We are not suggesting that you should adopt the role of artificially dripping with positivity. This won't work and you wouldn't be able to sustain it even if you were motivated to do so. There are two core confidence-building tactics that can be adopted here to good long-term effect. The first is to ensure that the team play to their strengths to achieve a strong positivity ratio, and the second is that they frame success and failure appropriately.

Playing to the team's strengths

We have already touched on the need to play to your individual strengths in previous chapters. However, a strengths focus at a team level can be a powerful way of building shared confidence. A good starting point here is to ensure you schedule time to talk to your team regularly about when they are at their best. At its simplest this can be a discussion of when the team members have felt at their best as a team, performing well and feeling good about it, and then exploring what characterizes these occasions. To what extent do the team feel that they are only at their best in response to particularly challenging circumstances? This can often be the initial response. However, it is usually worth probing to determine whether the team can identify where their actions create conditions that allow them to play to their strengths. Useful questions to pose here are:

- How do we (team members) interact with each other when we are at our best?
- What do we do to create opportunities that are likely to play to our strengths?
- Are there any differences in the types of work we tackle as a team when we are at our best in comparison to other times?
- Do we solve problems and deal with setbacks differently at our best? If so, what do we do?

If you want to extend this kind of approach it is worth looking at more formal techniques such as Appreciative Inquiry (AI) (Cooperrider *et al*, 2008). This has a structured four-stage approach: the 4-D Cycle:

Discovery – the best of what is, exploring when you are currently at your best collectively.

Dream – envisioning what the next level of success could look and feel like.

Design – co-creating the future to work towards the dream.

Destiny – embedding the change.

While AI is normally used in its full form as part of large change management programmes, the ethos behind it and its high level structure can be used regularly and informally.

Actively playing to your team's strengths is a way of replenishing the reservoir of shared positive experiences. It is also an important practical intervention to ensure the team functions to its full potential. Of course not everything is positive but we often don't do enough to ensure we achieve an accurate balance in terms of the attention we devote to positive and negative experiences. Without actively doing this we can end up with a distorted view of the team's effectiveness. Dwell on the positives, not just the negatives.

Rudyard Kipling's poem *If* is interesting in that it advocates that we should 'meet with Triumph and Disaster/And treat those two impostors just the same'. However, they are not the same and have different impacts on teams when they meet them. The sentiment behind Kipling's poem is the need to stay balanced and on an even keel, which is understandable. However, in our experience the risk in many organizations is that successes are rarely treated and understood as triumphs, while failures are often quickly labelled disasters. Successes are routinely discounted and the overriding emotional reaction to them often seems to be relief. Failures can easily be rapidly magnified until they feel like complete disasters.

Framing

We discussed the importance of framing relating to individual pressure experiences in the middle in Chapter 3. Framing is also important at the team level. Groups are often prone to biases and thinking errors when they evaluate issues. One bias that is particularly relevant to how teams can frame success and failure is the well-established group polarization (Lamm, 1988). This refers to the tendency for groups to evaluate issues and make decisions in a more extreme manner than the individuals involved would have done on their own. So imagine a team meeting where you are discussing something that has not gone well recently and has had a major impact on your progress as a team. It is likely that some people will be down about this and may start to postulate that it will have a larger impact on the team's work than it needs to. Unless this is challenged there is a high risk that the team will polarize around the view and allow it to magnify and negatively bias their decisions about what they should do next.

Inevitably when a team meets a setback they will not feel great about it. The challenge is to prevent this emotional reaction, and the conversations that are influenced by it, becoming self-fulfilling in terms of future team performance. It's important that the team doesn't drift into 'who' rather than 'what' thinking too frequently. Seeking to allocate blame within the team or beyond does little to help the team move on constructively from a setback. There are two strategies that are important here. The first is to question the postulated negative consequences in terms of whether they need to turn out as suggested and challenge the evidence base for the conclusions that are being drawn. The second is to remind the team that they are capable of dealing with setbacks and have probably done so successfully in the past.

At the end of this chapter we provide a guidance tool for maintaining and building team confidence. This includes both short-term (in the moment) and longer-term (time out) interventions. The only caveat worth adding is that, very occasionally, overconfidence can be a risk. Generally, we believe that boosting team confidence is important and that most team leaders and managers do not spend enough time actively doing so. Nevertheless, even positive qualities have upper limits. Overconfidence, and even hubris, are well-documented concerns among senior leaders, in particular the extent to which this contributed in the financial services industry to the conditions that created the 2007 crisis. However, high profile cases of board-level hubris in the banking sector do not mean that overconfidence is generally a major problem in organizations. This hubris, at its worst in this sector, is well-illustrated by Dowling and Lucey (2014: 8) in their review of behaviour and cognitive biases in the Irish banking sector in this period:

> we see that a degree of 'overconfidence being learned' is evident...
> A review of the 2007 Anglo Irish Bank annual report shows a very myopic perspective, with a large part of the CEO and Chairperson's reports devoted to discussion of recent success. Bank of Ireland were 'confident' of emerging stronger, Allied Irish had 'strength to meet the challenges'. All the Irish bank reports for 2007 display, in retrospect, an insouciance and overconfidence.

The issue seems to become most problematic when a state of inflated confidence leads to overly risky choices about future actions. It is important to differentiate between these two aspects. Confidence is a feeling: an emotional reaction. Decision making should not be too heavily influenced by emotional state, although there is an argument that it should not be entirely disconnected from it either. Therefore, confidence and decision making can be separated. So, if you do have concerns that your team are in an overconfident state perhaps the most important checkpoint is ensuring that they make balanced decisions that are not too heavily influenced by the fact that they may currently feel they can't do anything wrong! Overall this is probably a small risk for most people managing in the middle, trying to keep their team in a motivated and energized state.

Managing the pressure climate

Teams are frequently at their best under pressure. High pressure situations can stimulate innovation, raised performance and ultimately long-lasting positive emotions such as pride and increased respect for fellow team members. However, pressure needs to be managed to avoid stress and burn-out on the one hand and to ensure stretch and stimulation on the other.

In Chapter 2 we introduced the important distinction between challenge and hindrance pressures. The former are positive stretch pressures and the latter negative stressors. Both bring strain, but challenge pressures are linked to increased job satisfaction, organizational commitment and work performance, whereas heavy hindrance pressures are likely to produce negative outcomes in these areas. So, ideally, in a team we want to maximize challenge pressures and minimize hindrance ones. Of course which category pressures fall into is essentially determined by the perceptions of those exposed to them. However, one leadership response to this that we have seen fail frequently is to just encourage team members to see everything as a challenge. This won't work and it's inefficient. It won't work because it's inauthentic and will be interpreted as meaningless noise. It's inefficient because wasting time and energy on what might be genuine hindrance pressures, which you present as challenges, will block the team from making progress.

A strong starting point here is to host an open discussion with your team about what they see as challenges and hindrances. There are a number of reasons why this is useful. The first is to check your view against those of your team members. For example, do they discuss a pressure in hindrance terms when you believe it needs to be seen as a challenge? Another useful discovery is where you find disagreements among team members about whether a particular activity or task is perceived as a challenge or hindrance. These, particularly in relation to core teamwork activities, will have real implications for how team members work together. If one person feels an activity is important and believes he needs to devote a lot of time and energy to dealing with it (challenge pressure), and another feels it is largely a waste of time and she can't see the benefits of it (hindrance pressure), you have revealed a source of potential interpersonal difficulty. Even if this is not resulting in any real relationship problems it could still be creating inefficiency and frustration. The same activities and tasks can ultimately become challenges or hindrances in the minds of your team members. It is useful to develop a shared view of genuine hindrances: most teams in the middle of large organizations will have them. They tend to be system or process activities that may need to be carried out to serve some distant function in the organization but which have little or no obvious day-to-day benefit for the team's goals or aspirations. This does not mean that these things don't matter, but it makes clear that they are peripheral to the team and that they need to be controlled in terms of the time and energy devoted to them.

When you believe you have a goal or set of activities that you need your team to engage with properly as a challenge pressure and you believe they are seeing it or them as mainly a hindrance, how do you shift those perceptions? There are three aspects that appear to be important here to get people engaged in challenges and prevent them slipping back into the hindrance box: tangibility of results, control and feeling supported. We have already discussed the importance of these in the context of generally managing pressure in the middle. This means that to fully engage your team in a challenge it is worth asking yourself whether you can do more to help people see and feel what success would mean for them, whether they can control what they need to for goal achievement, and ensure they believe that they have support if they need it.

Wellbeing and performance

Leading your team to improve their wellbeing is a core way of building and sustaining high performance. Any notion that focusing on wellbeing weakens a performance orientation, or is in some way being soft with your people, is an outdated way of framing reality and flies in the face of a growing evidence base. Wellbeing is maximized when people perform at their best under pressure. This provides a deep positive emotional experience and strengthens purposefulness. When we suggest to some managers that they should manage the wellbeing of their people, they react in a way that suggests this is just another set of tasks they will have to do on top of managing performance. Managing for improved wellbeing at work does not mean focusing on a completely different set of factors than when managing for performance improvement. It is much more about how you manage these factors. Consider again the six key workplace factors that drive wellbeing in the ASSET model (Robertson and Cooper, 2011) we introduced in Chapter 2. Factors such as resources, workload, change and relationships are core drivers of performance just as much as they are wellbeing. In many ways, the active and open performance management of these factors with a team is the foundation for wellbeing. Of course it depends on the approach taken when doing so. Not surprisingly if you take an old style Theory X (McGregor, 1957) approach, based on the belief that your people can't be trusted to do the right thing and will need constant directing, you are unlikely to maximize wellbeing. Micromanagement is a very real threat to wellbeing. We will return to this below when we further consider the need to let go to enable your team to reach their potential.

A good starting point in placing an increased emphasis on wellbeing in your team is to carry out a simple wellbeing audit. This is best done using a valid categorization of work-related pressures, such as those in the ASSET model, or using the UK's Health and Safety Executive's management standards (2012) approach. It's then about understanding the pressure experience of your team members individually and collectively in these areas. Depending on the size and location of your team you may be able to do this through one-to-one and group conversations or you may need to collect some questionnaire data alongside this. Regardless of the outcomes this process itself can be very helpful. It signals to your team your intent to take their wellbeing seriously and it can reveal issues that have been simmering below the surface and which, if not addressed, have the potential to become bigger problems. Of course the outcomes are important, as is the follow-up to ensure action is taken to address any negative issues revealed and that you make the most of the positives. It really is critical that you follow up properly, particularly if team members are saying that some issues are causing them stress. In that case you may have a legal obligation to do so.

Once again the negative/positive balance is very important here. Just exploring everything that is wrong in terms of wellbeing isn't the right approach. However, nor is it sufficient just to find out where people are happy and wellbeing is positive. There are also other aspects that need to be considered in conducting a team wellbeing audit. Two worth emphasizing are the impact of pressures beyond the workplace and the possibility that you as the team manager are seen as a major source of stress!

Obviously when it comes to the wellbeing of your team you need to concentrate on the factors that influence this at work. This is where you will have most legitimate control. However, it can be a mistake to ignore the possibility that pressures outside of work may be having a significant impact that affects wellbeing and performance at work. This is an area that is best discussed one-to-one with team members. Usually this need be no more than a general enquiry about whether the individual has any problems at home or away from work that he or she feels have an impact on the work. If there are, you should then ask whether there is anything you or the organization can do to help or provide support. It is useful to know what support is available in your organization for employees with home difficulties (eg family relationship problems, debt, personal health issues) and to be able to signpost appropriate support when needed. Commonly this tends to be in the form of an Employee Assistance Programme (EAP).

You may have team members who believe that your management or leadership approach is a negative source of pressure for them. Probably the best way to deal with this possibility is to involve one of your peers, perhaps a manager at the same level from a different department, and ask him or her to act as a sounding board with your team concerning your impact. You can do this in an open way, inviting both positive feedback as well as any negative concerns they have. If this produces stronger concerns, for example if you are accused of bullying, then the issue should be dealt with using the appropriate organizational process, probably involving HR and a more senior manager.

When you have collected data on your team's wellbeing the next stage is to analyse and interpret it. If your team size is manageable we suggest this is best done openly in the spirt of sharing the interpretation of the results and co-creating solutions where required. Don't forget when doing this to pick out the key positives and discuss them.

The composition of your team and the extent to which they interact are important for both wellbeing and performance. You may lead a virtual team with members scattered geographically, possibly globally. Obviously this brings different challenges, particularly in terms of building and maintaining trust. If you lead a global team it is likely that the virtual nature of it will also mean you have team members from a range of different cultural backgrounds. Erez *et al* (2013) highlight two important core dimensions in teams like this and the relationship between these and trust: cultural intelligence (an individual's ability to reason well in situations of cultural diversity), and global identity (seeing a culturally diverse group as a single group or team). The former enables people to work well with differences and the latter to unify around similarities. Both of these are important for functional global teams. Trust plays a key role in terms of the likelihood of developing these qualities in the team. Building trust in virtual teams is more difficult than it is in teams with constant face-to-face interaction. As the interpersonal context is much weaker there tends to be a much heavier reliance on perceived reliability of delivery when judging trust. Therefore, if you lead a virtual team you need to place more emphasis than usual on ensuring people deliver what they say they will, particularly to each other.

Team development

There is a reasonably wide range of team development approaches. Perhaps the most frequently applied is the classic team away-day, taking your team out of the normal working environment in the hope they will relax and bond. Obviously these days, or sometimes longer events, take a variety of forms, including outdoor activity-based development, which can provide a powerful and unique experience for teams. There is some limited evidence that well-designed and executed programmes can make a lasting psychological difference in important areas such as self-efficacy (how effective people believe they are) (Propst and Koesler, 1998), and enhanced confidence in the effectiveness of the team facing difficult challenges (McEvoy and Cragun, 1997). However, these benefits are only achieved when the programme is well designed to meet the goals of the team undertaking it. The main issue with outdoor team development is transfer of learning back into the day-to-day working environment.

Taking your team away from the office environment occasionally either for team-building activities that are very different from their normal working activity or just for a discussion away from everyday pressures is probably a good idea. However, relying on this as your sole team development approach is almost certainly a bad idea. The most powerful team development is often that which occurs in real time on the job.

The team is your job

A key determinant of getting the best from your team is fully accepting that leading them is a core part of your job, and perhaps even the biggest part of it. This is something that we still see many middle managers struggling with. There are at least three role identities that can get in the way of this. The first is holding on too closely to an area of technical or specialist expertise; we discussed this in the last chapter in relation to the technical/functional career anchor. The second is seeing team leadership and management as a secondary role to your overall organizational one, by some distance. For example, if you are head of finance you concentrate most of your efforts on the organizational or business impact your function has rather than worrying about what your team are up to. Clearly there will be a balance to be struck here but we would always argue that managing and leading the team should receive at least the same amount of attention as positioning the function does.

It's worth acknowledging that we deliberately highlight both leading and managing your team. We discussed the leadership/management distinction back in Chapter 1 but in this context both are important. One way of thinking about this is to relate it to the challenge/hindrance pressure distinction previously mentioned. Hindrance pressures need to be managed if they are not to swamp the team. They need to be controlled and the team response to them should be structured and organized – key management activities. These may not always be very exciting but they are very necessary. Challenge pressures are a leadership opportunity: they require visioning, direction setting and inspiring people to rise to them. Leading challenge pressures without managing hindrance ones is risky, as sooner or later the hindrances will drag the team back from successfully meeting their challenges. Equally, just managing the hindrance pressures is insufficient. This might make life more comfortable for the team but without leading challenges they may cruise along in their comfort zone and not experience the wellbeing and performance benefits that come with stretch.

Stretch is important for teams. It enables them to raise their performance levels, build resilience and, ultimately, improve their wellbeing. However, by definition it can be difficult and uncomfortable. Stretch brings strain, and this needs to be managed. One of the most positive experiences in managing someone is when you work with them to meet a stretch challenge. Moving people from 'I don't believe I'm capable of this' to a position where they have succeeded in meeting the challenge can be transformational for them and very satisfying for you as their manager. This applies with individuals but probably even more so with teams. An essential ingredient in working through this process is balancing challenge and support, which we discussed above. Another, which overlaps with this, is building and maintaining team confidence (see the guidance tool at the end of the chapter).

The third role identity that can be a barrier here is when you see your role as a necessary evil on a path towards better or different things. Obviously there is nothing wrong with having an ambition to be promoted further or take on a different role at the same level. However, if you just tolerate leading or managing your team, or have a prime motivation of being seen from above as leading your team effectively, you will almost certainly run into trouble. This kind of manipulation is soon obvious and damages credibility and trust.

Letting go – allowing the team to fail

It usually feels counter-intuitive to allow your team to fail. However, we would argue that allowing them to do so from time to time can ultimately have a very positive impact on their long-term performance and wellbeing. It's about giving them space to solve problems and meet challenges without jumping in and being directive every time you believe they are going off track. Obviously this isn't always easy to do, and there will be times when the risks are too high and you need to intervene. But, if you always jump in, you are behaving like an overly-protective parent, the result of which is usually a dependency mode of operation that actually prevents effective team-working and development. We highlighted near the start of this chapter that interdependence is an essential condition for team-working. Developing this state means you have to be ready to stop exerting too much direct control. It's also important for helping the team feel they have the levels of control they need to operate effectively – improving their wellbeing and performance. When managers fail to let go and give their team enough operational space there are usually a few common justifications that we regularly hear from them, such as:

'I need to stay close to what they are doing as I'm the one that's being held accountable for their performance.'

'The only way I can be sure they will stay focused is by staying directly involved.'

'They just don't have enough experience yet to operate without frequent direction from me.'

These can seem reasonable in the moment when facing heavy delivery pressures, particularly to the managers themselves, and often their boss. However, if they become default motivations they usually need to be challenged. So here are some challenge questions/observations that could be tabled in response to such assertions:

'Accountability does not mean that you shouldn't delegate responsibility. You can give people more space and still set expectations about keeping you up to date with how they are doing against their objectives from time to time.'

'Perhaps you being on their back all the time is a major reason that they lose focus on the task and their goals?'

'How will they get more experience if you jump in and take problems from them whenever it looks like they might struggle?'

At an extreme level this can be micromanagement: a tendency that ultimately leaves teams, and individuals, feeling powerless and not trusted to do their job. The key here is recognizing if you have a strong need for control, or tend to find it difficult to trust others, and then learning to manage this so that it doesn't become micromanagement.

Influencing beyond your team

In this chapter we have concentrated on the influence and impact you can have with your team. However, managing in the middle means you have to be able to influence on a number of different fronts. This can seem daunting, but it is also a core source of power and impact that is more difficult for those at more junior, and indeed more senior, positions to exert. It is much easier to sustain a positive influence beyond your team when you do so from a strong base of being happy with where you have your own team. In the next two chapters we will consider the two other main points of influence that will be important to you in the middle. In Chapter 7 we will consider influencing and managing upwards, but first we turn to the influence and impact you can have on your peers – those at the same level in the hierarchy.

GUIDANCE TOOL

Team confidence builder

Figure 5.1 Building team confidence

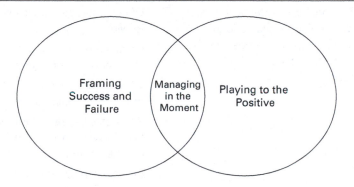

As described above, both framing success and failure appropriately, and playing to the positive and strengths, are the foundations for building and maintaining team confidence. However, these shouldn't be seen as discrete activities that are applied through team-building programmes on a one-off or very occasional basis, but as aspects that need to be managed consistently and appropriately in the moment. There is a place for concentrated time-out development activity every now and again but it is arguably more important to view the management of confidence as something that should be a continuous priority. A Google search on 'team confidence building exercises' reveals a wide array of games and exercises. These have their place, but we believe confidence ebbs and flows regularly and a team leader often needs to intervene when it is going in the wrong direction at the moment it is happening, rather than waiting for the next team away-day. This doesn't mean you always need to be ready to jump in and be very directive (note the earlier warning about micromanagement) when you sense team confidence is waning. The action you take can, and often should, be quite subtle, a bit like gently moving the tiller of a yacht rather than tearing the sails down and starting the engine. Taking over in a heavy-handed way is likely to send messages that further dent team confidence rather than bolster it.

Tables 5.3 and 5.4 provide suggestions for both framing success and failure and playing to the positive quickly in the moment and at more intensive (time-out) interventions. Often a quick intervention in the moment will be all that's required to maintain and bolster team confidence. However, when you believe this has been deeply affected, a more detailed longer intervention may be required.

Table 5.3 Framing success and failure

Managing in the moment	Time out interventions
Success	**Success**
• Acknowledge the success and the roles everyone played in achieving it. • Challenge any tendency to move on too quickly: encourage the team to linger in the positive emotions associated with success.	• Analyse what the team did to achieve the success, asking questions like: What obstacles did we overcome to win through? When were we at our best in striving towards our goals? Where were we particularly effective in collaborating? What can we learn from this and take forward to increase our chances of future success? • Discuss and agree how to communicate the success beyond the team boundary.
Failure	**Failure**
• Listen for escalation or magnification of the failure beyond what has actually happened. Challenge this and ask for evidence for such assertions. • Challenge any tendency to immediately look to blame or label people when things go wrong.	• Analyse what went wrong but without seeking to attach blame. Realistically consider what the team could have done differently as well as acknowledging any factors outside their control. Highlight that hindsight is 20:20 and some things that go wrong can only be seen after the fact. • Draw a line under the failure. Spend time looking forward to your next major challenge.

Table 5.4 Playing to the positive

Managing in the moment	Time-out interventions
'Catch them doing something right': genuinely express your pleasure in excellent performance when it occurs. You don't have to do this every time: it's actually more powerful done genuinely and occasionally. Highlight where you believe the team has made positive progress, particularly when you believe they are losing sight of this. Start regular meetings by sharing where things are going well.	Encourage team members to share what they see as their colleagues' strengths and to reinforce the positive impact they have. Just have fun: do something completely unrelated to normal team activity. Find an opportunity for team members to relax and just enjoy each other's company away from normal work pressures.

Influencing and working with your peers   06

In this chapter we focus on influencing your same-level peers and working effectively with them. We start by discussing why this is important and the nature of peer influence and relationships. We then consider how you can learn from your peers and we focus on how working well with them facilitates effective decision making. We consider the true nature of how information flows in organizations and the role you can play in this in middle management. We show how you can shape and influence strategy by working well with your colleagues in the middle, as well as how your collective middle management power can shape and define working experience across the organization.

The traditional hierarchical organization places an emphasis on managing and influencing downwards as well as working effectively upwards, but very little on what happens sideways. The changing nature of many organizational forms suggests this perspective is outdated and limited. For example, matrix-like structures place as much emphasis on working relationships horizontally as vertically and these structures have multiple lines of responsibility and accountability. Middle managers can operate effectively in such organizations but only when they have a network of relationships that they can draw on to help them navigate through the complexity.

There are a number of reasons why influencing your peers and building strong relationships at the same level in the hierarchy is very important in a mid-level position; among the most important are:

- building a strong support network;

- learning from your peers;

- getting things done effectively;

- better understanding and influencing distributed, multiple-stakeholder decision making;

- having a real impact on the strategic direction of your organization;

- shaping organizational reality through collective middle management.

We discuss each of these themes and others in this chapter, although they overlap significantly. However, before exploring these we start by considering what we can learn from the psychology of peer influence generally that is likely to be particularly useful from a mid-level position.

Peer influencing and networking

Peer influence has significantly different characteristics to managerial or subordinate influence. A meta-analysis study over a decade ago (Higgins *et al*, 2003), pulling together a large number of research studies, highlighted two peer influencing approaches that have a demonstrable impact on work performance – ingratiation and rationality. Ingratiation is behaving in a deliberately friendly manner or doing whatever is necessary to be liked. This may be a quality that is not attractive to many, but that doesn't mean it's ineffective. Rationality in this context is using data or logic to try to persuade and influence. It is feasible that these approaches may work better among same-level peers than in a cross-hierarchy level way. For example, trying to ingratiate yourself with your manager may be viewed with greater suspicion than seeking to do so with a colleague at the same level. Likewise, when there is no hierarchical difference perhaps rationality becomes more important, as formal status is less obvious and influential. When position power is less obvious it is likely that influencing on the basis of a solid, evidence-based argument should carry more weight overall.

Ingratiation may seem a somewhat contentious interpersonal approach but there may be times when this is exactly what you need to do with your peers. In particular, where a relationship has been neglected or when you believe the other person has a distorted perception of you, ingratiation may be the right strategy. We certainly wouldn't recommend overreliance on such an approach. However, it is naive to think that you should never adopt it or that it never works. Being openly friendly beyond what you normally display and trying your hardest to be likeable may be necessary from time to time and may open up new relationship opportunities. Of course there needs to be substance and authenticity behind this if it is not to be dismissed, or end up as a counter-productive suspicion of motives. For example, if you are trying to influence a fellow middle manager who has a reputation for being difficult to get close to, a combination of ingratiation and rationality may be the best approach. You may need to be openly friendly initially to a greater extent than you would typically, but blend this with some early well-founded arguments to really get their attention.

There will be times when a data-driven logical approach is generally the best way to influence your peers effectively. Building a reputation as someone who takes an objective evidence-based approach could provide a strong platform as a peer influencer. When faced with complexity and too many demands, having a same-level colleague to consult who will help you take a logical analytical approach to key problems is very valuable. However, there is a risk of overusing this kind of style and being labelled as a 'techie' or being seen as lacking emotional empathy – the excessive reliance on any single influencing approach has a downside.

To build long-term peer relationships, influence almost certainly needs to be shared. A useful concept here is 'reciprocal credits' (McIntosh and Luecke, 2011). When you do a good deed for one of your peers you earn a credit that you can cash in when you need support. Of course it is unlikely to be that literal, or credit by credit reciprocal, but the principle holds up. There is a strong rationale for this being particularly important in mid-level roles. When you are facing a barrage of demands from above and below you need a strong drive to help out a same-level colleague. If it is someone who has regularly supported you, you are much more likely to reciprocate even though you are already overloaded. Engaging in this authentically can't be sustained in a deliberately manipulative way. Generally doing good deeds for your peers is beneficial for your wellbeing as well as boosting the likelihood of receiving support from them when you need it. If this becomes something you do for its own sake you build reciprocal credits without realizing it or it feeling like a chore or task.

When thinking about your peer network it's important to consider what may attract your peers to you as well as what you actively do to initiate and try to build relationships with them. An interesting take on this is provided by Levinson and Mann (2009) in their book *Guerrilla Networking*. They argue that the key to effective networking is to behave in a way that is likely to attract others to you, rather than spending most of your time trying to work out ways to meet those that are appealing to you. It's a pull rather than push approach to networking. They go on to suggest no less than 50 ways to attract people to you. Some of these are more relevant to broad external networking than to internal peer networking, and it is not always clear that there is evidence for the success of all of the approaches. However, it is the mindset that Levinson and Mann are arguing for that is worth considering. They advocate that uniqueness is the key quality in becoming someone that attracts others to you. This is an important consideration if you are in a middle management position in a large complex business or organization. What do your peers see in you that they don't see in others? What value can you add to your peers that differentiates you, and can't be easily replicated by others? These are key questions we will explore further below.

Another interesting point made by Levinson and Mann is that being an effective networker requires an openness in terms of allowing others to help and support you: the relationship is strengthened by welcoming support as well as by giving it. Supporting others helps us feel better about ourselves. This also fits with the reciprocal currency idea. If you just do good things for others but don't accept their help, it's not a reciprocal arrangement. Asking your peers for help when you need it may be just as important as offering help in terms of strengthening long-term relationships. Essentially the argument is for an openness of attitude and being prepared to admit when you need support as well as considering how you can provide it. This requires an emotional maturity and self-confidence in the sense that you are comfortable admitting you need support from time to time.

In previous chapters we have discussed the benefits of having a strong support network and of networking as a career development activity. However, there are more immediate reasons for building a strong peer-level network. The first is to facilitate getting things done in a large complex organization. It's unlikely that you will only need to exert an influence in a vertical direction within your function or department. The nature of influence and decision making in many organizations is distributed, and sometimes quite chaotic. Therefore, being effective and getting results often means working across organizational boundaries. This is much easier when you have a strong peer-level network that you can utilize when the need arises.

If you face a challenging project or assignment, particularly one that is broad and cross-functional, drawing on a strong peer network is very important. This may be task-related in that you ask a colleague for direct help to undertake an activity. However, it can be just as useful to call on your peers for useful intelligence, regardless of whether they have a direct involvement in the work you are undertaking. Drawing on the experience and tacit knowledge of colleagues is an advantage. Sometimes this may provide you with a fresh perspective or new insight; at other times it may just be useful for checking your own frame of reference with someone else whose opinion you value. In this way you can informally learn and develop while solving day-to-day problems. To a large extent this will be the most effective form of peer learning, but there is often a case for organizing a more structured form of this.

Learning from your peers

There are many ways to learn and develop in organizational life. We believe that peer-to-peer learning is among the most powerful. Your colleagues at the same level as you in the middle of the organizational hierarchy have multiple sources of relevant knowledge available to them and share an awareness of the context you are operating within. Peer mentoring can be particularly effective; there is some evidence that it can facilitate knowledge creation as well as sharing (Bryant, 2005).

Effective and sustainable peer mentoring relationships normally require a number of conditions. The first, and probably the most important, is that both parties need to be able to draw benefits from the relationship. Peer mentoring should be a true exchange of value, on a reasonably equitable basis. If one person feels he or she is gaining a lot for his or her development but the other doesn't, it's unlikely to be sustained in a way that is satisfying to both. The second condition is that there is a roughly equal divide in terms of the time devoted to the issues of each person. This requires good active listening, and an understanding that you may be able to gain almost as much from supporting the other person as from talking about your own problems. This latter aspect should be particularly true in a peer relationship. Understanding the experience and perspective of your colleague can widen your knowledge base and is likely to be very relevant to the challenges you face. Connected to this is the need to adopt a clear structure for your peer mentoring conversations, particularly in the early stages of the relationship, when it is often best to divide equally the time you spend discussing each person's issues in a fairly rigid manner. This means you are either in the role of talking about the issues you face or primarily in the mentor role and listening and reflecting. Doing this helps to ensure the time you spend together doesn't just become a series of general conversations with neither party very clear on what they are drawing from the exchanges.

Your organization may have a peer mentoring scheme and, if so, accessing this could be the right channel to pursue. However, there is nothing to stop you approaching one of your peers and asking whether he or she is interested in exploring a mutually beneficial mentoring arrangement. In doing so you should be ready to state your objectives upfront and ask your potential buddy to consider his or hers. It's probably best to informally contract a trial period and expectations for the relationship: perhaps a three-month trial, agreeing to meet or talk every couple of weeks. You should also be clear upfront about it being fine for either party at the end of this period to terminate the arrangement if it is not really working. It's probably best to choose someone who you have limited day-to-day contact with but at roughly the same hierarchical level in the business or organization.

A couple of decades ago the term 'learning organization' was adopted by many, following the 1990 publication of Peter Senge's book *The Fifth Discipline*. The term is less often heard these days but many of the principles still hold true, and we believe peer-to-peer learning is underutilized as a mechanism for improving the learning culture in many organizations. One aspect that Senge (1990) emphasizes that is particularly relevant here, is the link to mastery. He writes:

> People with a high level of personal mastery live in a continual learning mode. They never 'arrive'. Sometimes, language, such as the term 'personal mastery' creates a misleading sense of definiteness, of black and white. But personal mastery is not something you possess. It is a process. It is a lifelong discipline. People with a high level of personal mastery are acutely aware of their ignorance, their incompetence, and their growth areas. And they are deeply self-confident. Paradoxical? Only for those who do not see the 'journey' is the reward. (1990: 142)

This seems to be particularly important from a middle management or mid-level perspective. If you accept that the middle is where you are likely to spend the rest of your career (and of course you may not), and you want that to be a fulfilling period in your life, mastery becomes a critical source of satisfaction and wellbeing. This brings a fresh perspective on peer learning. If you adopt a position where life-long learning is your raison d'être, then engaging fully with your peers to help you, and them, achieve mastery will be very positive in its impact. There is almost certainly still a need to be fairly clear about what you want to master (eg technical expertise, business acumen, interpersonal leadership). Describing an experience as a journey has become a bit clichéd, thanks to too many reality TV shows, but it is an accurate description of development with a mastery ethos.

Better understanding and influencing distributed decision making

Decision making, particularly when the decisions are strategic, is rarely just a top-down hierarchical process in large organizations. It's a distributed and shared activity and middle managers and leaders have a key role to play in this. From a middle position you can often make a stronger contribution by working with your peers at the same level. In their review of the interface between the top management team and middle managers, Raes *et al* (2011) highlight that the inter-actions between these levels are often limited and too constrained in scope, and as a result can have a negative impact on strategic decision quality. Managing these relationships upwards is the focus of the next chapter, but strengthening peer relationships at middle levels may have an important role to play here. Working collaboratively across the organization at mid-levels can serve to improve strategy formation and implementation as well as enabling a collectivist approach to engaging upwards.

Strategic direction is normally set from the top. However, the interpretation of this and translation into implementation activity is where mid-level leaders and managers play a key role. Doing this without collaborating across functions inevitably results in at best patchy, and at worst completely inconsistent, implementation. Consulting with your peers to build a shared understanding of how strategic change should be implemented is likely to lead to better results as well as being intrinsically rewarding. For example, say your role is head of a major sales team and a strategic change in direction requires you to sell services rather than products. You could just try to work out how to do this on your own and get on with implementing it. But how much more effective are you likely to be if you consult your peers in HR and marketing? A change such as this has implications in terms of the composition of your team and their development (requires HR involvement) and in terms of understanding how the service proposition is being marketed and what it means for branding (marketing input required). Equally your colleagues in these functions will benefit from working closely with you to understand the implications in their areas. It's possible this collaboration may occur through structured processes but this may not be enough. Informal discussions are just as important and allow a more open and natural conversation about what the change really means in practice.

In the last couple of decades a significant amount of research has examined distributed decision making in organizational systems. As communication had become easier and faster, empowerment through organizations has become commonplace, the traditional power structures have changed, and decision making has generally become less centralized and involved more players. Malone (1997) argues that the extent to which decision making is decentralized and distributed is dependent on three main factors: decision information, trust and motivation. Consider these from a mid-level peer working perspective:

- *Decision information* – from a mid-level position you should have ready 360-degree access to key information for taking strategically important decisions. Of course accessing this may not always be easy, but a strong peer network is an important enabler of doing so.

- *Trust* – strong relationships with your peers provide a stable basis for collaborative and open decision making. Trust also tends to speed up decision making as people are less likely to waste time wondering about the motivations of their peers, or playing politics rather than working together to reach solutions.

- *Motivation* – distributed decision making only becomes a reality when people are committed to collaborating to make the best possible decision. Clearly all decisions don't need to be made in this way and trying to do so wastes time. However, complex decisions require the drive to involve all those who can bring an important contribution. Working openly with your colleagues to solve difficult problems can lead to interactions that are motivating and stimulating. It can also help you build a reputation as a true team player and someone who seeks to do what's best for the collective rather than just individually.

In global organizations peer level distributed decision making may mean working cross-culturally. The notion of power distance introduced in Chapter 1 is important here. Cultures with a high power distance are less likely to have open distributed decision making as a norm in comparison to those lower in power distance. Therefore, working across such cultural differences requires sensitivity and a different negotiation approach when discussing involvement in collective strategic decision making. For example, in a high power-distance culture you will need to reassure upwards that middle level collaboration need not threaten the hierarchy or position of those at the most senior level. Transparency of intent will be far more important than in a low power-distance culture.

One role that is critically important in distributed decision making is challenging possible cognitive biases. In mid-level positions there is a reasonable chance that you work with peers with a similar background to you and with whom you share many assumptions and values. This can be positive in terms of providing a basis for establishing strong relationships, but it can also serve to increase the likelihood of cognitive biases regularly influencing decision making. Understanding the impact of cognitive biases has developed from the pioneering work of Tversky and Kahneman (1974), which showed that decision making does not always follow rational pathways and is influenced by irrational error tendencies. These biases often occur facing challenges that are new, important, involve a high level of uncertainty, and arise under high levels of time pressure. This might seem like every day from a middle management perspective.

One interesting finding relating to distributed decision making is that teams have a bias towards overreacting to incorrect information early in the decision process in comparison to any that emerges later (Mancuso et al, 2014). Perhaps this is related to the pressure to find instant solutions to difficult problems. Organizations often reward decisiveness, and those who make quick decisions can be thought of as dynamic and action-oriented. However, there are times when acting in haste can leave you repenting at leisure and there is a need to slow down decision making. For example, if you need to make decisions that are likely to shape your year ahead, such as year-start budgeting or resource allocation decisions, this is probably a time to slow down and ensure you have considered all of the important factors. Yet how often as a middle manager have you been involved in a year end/start frenzy where there is constant time pressure to sign off accounts, plans and budgets? This often leads to ill-considered plans and budgets that are quickly exposed as such.

A high pressure environment increases the likelihood of a strong bias that occurs in both individual and group decision making: confirmation bias. When we believe we have found a credible solution to a problem there is a strong tendency to give too much weight to evidence that confirms our view and dismiss information that may suggest we are wrong. Interestingly, being an expert in an area does not necessarily reduce the probability of this bias occurring and, in some circumstances, may increase it. For example, Legoux *et al* (2014), when investigating how IT experts estimated the financial impact of IT innovations, found that the more expert they were the greater the confirmation bias. They also found this risk could be reduced when the evaluation was undertaken by a group with more diverse expertise.

In practice, this suggests that working with a wide range of peers when facing complex problems should help to reduce error and lead to better decisions. It highlights that there is a need to challenge the direction that groups and teams seem to be taking, particularly in the early stages of decision making. The form of this challenge should be to encourage all involved to consider other possibilities and perspectives. One technique that is useful is to encourage the evaluation of the polar opposite solution to the one that seems to be gaining consensus, before making a full commitment to that solution. Time put into challenging each other about conclusions drawn early in a process is likely to be well spent. Doing this effectively is partially dependent on trust and the overall strength of the relevant interpersonal relationships. Investing in building a strong peer network will have a payback in allowing you to challenge without meeting excessive defensive reactions too frequently. Without this relationship bedrock, your peers are much more likely to see challenge as threat. This can be a real hindrance when trying to make important decisions and can lead to relationships increasingly characterized by suspicion and political behaviour.

Organizational network analysis

One area of research that throws some light on the importance of relationships is the relatively new field of organizational network analysis (Novak *et al*, 2011). This approach maps relationship networks in organizations and how they function in terms of actual information flow and decision making. They allow us to visualize this flow and better understand how people really interact as opposed to how the formal positional structure would suggest they should. An interesting finding, particularly for those in mid-level roles, is that different individuals tend to adopt different information flow roles in networks. For example, 'central connectors' tend to serve as core exchange hubs and have the highest number of direct connections in the network. If you play this role you are probably seen as the go-to person by others when they are uncertain about where to access information or key knowledge sources. This could be very beneficial in terms of career progression because your utility is likely to be visible across the organization as you will be readily thought of as a key player in the function of the business or organization. There will also be day-to-day advantages in terms of getting things done when support is required. Obviously there are risks of becoming swamped and overloaded with requests for information or access to other knowledge sources.

There are other roles in networks revealed by this approach that are just as critical. One that is very relevant is the 'information broker'. This role is one that broadly links networks across boundaries and locations. It's a role that enables distributed decision making across a widely spread and diverse set of networks rather than within one recognizable single network. For example, say you are head of research and development for a pharmaceutical company and readily play the information broker role. To enable your company to stay at the scientific leading edge you can readily connect your network within your organization to professional bodies in related areas such as medical associations, global health thought leaders, and world-leading universities and think tanks. You feed information and knowledge into these networks from your own organization and ensure the connections are in place to allow a flow back in from the various networks you are connected with. You actively engineer the links and interconnections to ensure information and knowledge are curated and brokered in a way that maximizes benefits for your business, as well as bringing personal wins. Someone playing this role will have a career currency that is recognized well beyond their own organizations – your reciprocal currency is Euros rather than Pounds Sterling!

Going open source

The information broker would probably thrive in an open source environment. Open source computing has grown enormously in the last decade and allows open access to code and collaborative open development of software. Some have embraced this, seeing it as providing freedom to work and develop knowledge without reliance on closed established power bases. Others tend to see it as chaotic and dangerous. This is an interesting analogy when thinking about your preferences when working with peers and people at similar levels within your organization and beyond it. Are you an open source type who will naturally expose your work to your peers, unfinished and probably full of errors, and allow the peer network to use it and take it to new places? Or does this thought fill you with dread: you'd be very unlikely to share your work until it was in a polished, finished form? The latter approach has traditionally been valued and rewarded to a much greater extent than the former, but perhaps this is changing. Perhaps the closed source approach has promoted a secrecy-obsessed, overcontrolling empire-building culture that has had its time.

To operate in an open source collaborative mode requires a lot of confidence. It requires a belief that errors and imperfection are necessary components of development and improvement. It can only really take hold in a climate short on blame. To function like this in a non-supportive culture would be brave, but possibly naive. However, being open with your peers is likely to encourage a similar response. There will be some who seek to exploit and blame – but in the long term that's their problem!

Strategy influencing and formation

From a mid-level position in large organizations the role you can play in influencing and forming strategy is very significant. Peer collaboration plays a critical role in this. Middle managers play a key role in the successful implementation of strategic direction. In turning direction into new activities and behaviours, middle managers define and formulate strategy in action. To do this in a way that is well informed and ultimately successful, collaborative peer working is required. Cross-functional work is needed to formulate strategic implementation with sufficient breadth and specificity. Sull *et al* (2015) discuss this in the context of distributed leadership and the middle manager's role:

> Distributed leaders, not senior executives, represent 'management' to most employees, partners, and customers. Their day-to-day actions, particularly how they handle difficult decisions and what behaviors they tolerate, go a long way toward supporting or undermining the corporate culture. (p 10)

They go on to highlight, based on extensive survey data, that middle managers are often seen as authentic in terms of how they reflect the organization: 'As assessed by their direct reports, more than 90% of middle managers live up to the organization's values all or most of the time' (Sull *et al*, 2015: 10). Therefore, developing a shared view on strategy with your middle management colleagues is critical in terms of defining strategy and implementing it in a credible and meaningful way. Clearly it is easiest to achieve this in a climate where senior executives expect and reward such an active and collaborative response to strategic priorities. As Sull and his colleagues highlight, this may be espoused but rarely truly enabled, particularly in terms of what gets rewarded. They argue that so long as managers perform against their main quantifiable goals, 'hit their numbers', they are unlikely to be penalized for not properly collaborating with their peers to create broader strategic implementation, which may be much more important in the long term:

> We ask respondents what would happen to a manager in their organization who achieved his objectives but failed to collaborate with colleagues in other units. Only 20% believe the behavior would be addressed promptly; 60% believe it would be addressed inconsistently or after a delay, and 20% believe it would be tolerated. (Sull *et al*, 2015: 9)

(We will come back to this issue in the next chapter in terms of managing upwards.) The impact of this is likely to be negative in terms of your collaborative efforts. However, you should consider the risks of not sufficiently working collaboratively with your peers. One is clearly that you are not adding to your bank of reciprocal credits, and that when the time comes that you need support from your peers you may find they have other priorities.

Peer support networks

Generally, building a strong peer network will be good for your wellbeing. There is a long tradition in work and organizational psychology of seeking to understand the causes and effects associated with the healthy, happy, productive worker. In recent years this has been expanded to the healthy, happy, *connected,* productive worker. The social side of wellbeing is now being recognized more explicitly than it ever has. This applies to all areas of our lives but work is certainly among the most important. You may feel that you have all the support you need away from work, or that you are very independent at work and don't rely on others for support. This is risky for a couple of reasons. You may well have lots of great support away from work and this will often be very helpful. However, as we suggested in Chapter 3, there are definitely times when the most useful support is that which comes from those who have a full understanding of the context of the problems and challenges you face. This is much more likely to be your peers than your family. In reality this peer support will only be readily accessible if you actively develop your peer network, even at times when you don't feel the need for much support. You should think through what you do to develop this as an end in itself, without necessarily having ulterior task motives. This could include informal and social contact for its own sake. This is not explicit self-promotion: it is self-enhancement through deepening important relationships. Others will often appreciate a genuine approach just to find out how they are doing and catch up without an explicit task motive.

One approach that can serve the dual purposes of strengthening peer support and solving important business problems is the use of action learning sets. These have a long history as organizational interventions and can be very powerful. Essentially they are groups of peers working together to solve problems. They follow a set sequence of reflection, planning, acting and reflecting again. Participants bring real problems to the group and they work together to analyse the issues and suggest possible solutions. This can be really beneficial when structured effectively and the discipline of the process is followed. If you have not already used this approach in your organization, it may be worth finding out more about it and trying it. Pedler (2008) provides a useful and practical guide to action learning for managers.

Using peer networks to manage hindrance pressures

In Chapter 2 we introduced the distinction between negative hindrance and positive challenge pressures, and revisited this in the context of getting the best from your team in Chapter 5. Having a strong peer network can help you control hindrance pressures and free up time and resource to rise to challenges. When we ask groups of managers at all levels across many different types of businesses and organizations about their hindrance pressures we are often struck by the similarities rather than differences. Three of the most common are: too many e-mails, too many or badly run meetings, and bureaucratic systems or processes. So what can you do with your middle management peers to control these?

E-mails

You may be able to remember a time when if you wanted to communicate broadly across the organization you would write a memo. You would have to carefully consider who should receive it. You probably took some time to compose your message and word it just right, and you would usually state very clearly what action was required. Compare this to bashing out an e-mail in a few minutes, sending it to those you immediately think need to see it, but copying in many of your peers 'for information'. It's not difficult to see how the latter is much more likely to drive information overload and misunderstanding than the former. Of course, it would be naive to suggest we should go back to posted communication and abandon all electronic forms. In Chapter 3 we discussed strategies for individually dealing with e-mail overload, but working with your peers to address this pan-organizationally may be more effective. For example, you could host a discussion with a number of your mid-level colleagues about how e-mail is used in the organization and agree an informal protocol to reduce the volume of largely unnecessary or ineffective e-mails. One key to this is to consider three reasons people tend to overuse e-mail and how you as a group of influential people in the organization should respond to these:

1 *Uncertainty about who should be cc'd into an e-mail:* this is often the result of a lack of clarity regarding information flow and responsibilities. We have noted above that this can be complex and blurred in many organizations. However, a group of mid-level peers is probably better placed than anyone else to steer others on where there are critical information paths and where perhaps there is little need to disseminate more information just in case others need to see it. This is not an easy problem to solve but middle managers are better placed than anyone else to try to address it. They will do so most effectively if they collaborate with their peers to advise others consistently in this respect.

2 *Covering your back:* this is political behaviour – a typical example is to copy in your manager on an e-mail just so that he or she can see that you have done your bit. This should be challenged. Agreeing with your peers that you will challenge team members who seem to frequently copy you or others into their e-mails to cover their backs is an important culture change lever. The challenge can be as simple as asking the individual why he or she thought that you (or another party) needed to see a particular e-mail. You can do this without consulting your peers but it will have a bigger impact on the organization if there is a consistent middle management behavioural response here.

3 *Conflict avoidance:* trying to deal with sensitive issues through e-mail is nearly always less effective than having a face-to-face conversation. It is also easy to start a conflict via e-mail if you are not careful. You are short of time and you write a brief direct e-mail message to one of your colleagues. He or she interprets this as being abrupt or rude and fires back a tetchy response – and we are off into an increasingly immature flame-mail exchange. The solution is a conversation as soon as possible. Whenever there is an issue that is contentious or sensitive, e-mail will almost certainly be the wrong medium to use to address it. Recognizing this with your peers will lead to more open and successful cross-functional communication and again serve to provide a consistent positive cultural influence.

Meetings

Middle managers are probably as guilty as most of overvaluing meetings. Obviously meetings can be useful, but we often expect too much from them or default to them whenever a new problem appears. For example, we know from research that problem solving in groups is difficult, particularly when more than about seven people are involved. So if you spend hours and hours in large meetings with colleagues trying to solve problems it's likely to be less than optimal. Meetings like this need to be well structured and run if they are going to succeed. There are probably a number of challenges here that a middle management group could collectively lead to positive effect, such as:

- Being clear on the need for a meeting. Avoiding slipping into custom and practice mode, eg 'We always have this meeting' without occasionally challenging why, and what it should be achieving.

- Having a shared understanding of the basic expectations when calling and running meetings (eg always leaving meetings with shared clarity and agreement on any actions required).

- Agreeing not to overschedule back-to-back meetings that sap concentration, energy and productivity.

Bureaucratic systems

Middle managers are also best placed to challenge and change bureaucratic systems and processes. They should have an obvious rationale for their existence and detailed requirements for their completion. Senior managers should have an understanding of the rationale, but may not be familiar with their operational detail. In contrast more junior people will have the operational familiarity but may lack an appreciation of the rationale for what they are engaged with. With your peers in the middle you have the knowledge and reach to improve systems and processes and mitigate the risk of them being perceived as negative hindrances. To achieve this, you will need to agree with your peers which systems and processes most need attention and find some time to review them and agree what is required. This will almost certainly be time well spent. In some cases, it may be a communication rather than system change problem that needs to be addressed. For example, have some more junior people lost sight of the importance of some systems or processes and need to be re-engaged to appreciate this better? In other cases you may conclude fundamental change is required and that a business case needs to be made for doing so. If this is necessary, you should be able to collectively build such a case and convince senior executives to support it much more effectively than trying to do so in individual isolation.

Working with your peers for outstanding middle management

One of our core objectives in this book is to positively reframe middle management. The last section about hindrance pressures is a strong illustration of why this is so important. If you sit in the middle in a large organization, you have both management and leadership responsibilities. In our experience the latter have tended to be emphasized to a greater extent than the former in the last 20 years. However, we believe that day-to-day management is at least as important, and perhaps more so, than leadership. You should lead in terms of playing a role to set direction and try to motivate and inspire people to follow this. However, in the middle you will spend more time managing than leading, and this is where your true power lies. Managing – organizing, controlling and monitoring activity – is crucial for business and organizational success. This is no less important now; in fact, there is an argument that with changing and looser organizational forms, management has never been more important.

As a middle manager you have the power to define the reality of experience across the organizational hierarchy, and to have as large an impact of effective functioning as more senior executives. You can exercise that power individually but it will really be unleashed when you work well with your peers at the same level. Taking the time and effort to build and maintain the relationships to do so will pay off in multiples. The pay-offs will not just be increased productivity and performance but also enhanced motivation and wellbeing.

Improving the way you work with your peers

Given the ground we have covered in this chapter, how can you use this to work more effectively with your peers and strengthen your network for outstanding middle management? The starting point is to specify your goals in this respect. These are likely to be a mix of short- and longer-term goals and objectives. Table 6.1 contains some suggested prompts to help you capture these. Once you have some goal clarity you need to define your contact strategy. Key considerations here are:

- How do I approach this person in a way that will add value for both of us?

- To reach out to someone I don't know well, is there someone I know who also knows him or her who can facilitate an introduction?

- Are there any cross-functional groups or events I can attend that could be helpful?

Table 6.1 Improving the way you work with your peers

Short term – proximal sphere of influence	Longer term – wider sphere of influence
• Who are your closest peers in terms of your organization's structure and how strong is your relationship with them? • Are there current projects or responsibilities you have which might benefit from more input from your peers? • Do you face any important decisions that could be informed by more input from your peers?	• How strong is your peer network – who could you rely on if you needed support? Who can you have a safe conversation with? • What might you learn from peers you don't interact with regularly? • Is there anyone you know who has a good reputation at a similar level to you, but you don't know them well? How could you get to know them better? • What broad challenges do you and your same level peers share and how can you improve your interaction to address them?

Consider all avenues that are open to you to engage more frequently and effectively with your peers across the organization. However, you need to prioritize your activity around your goals. Don't be too ambitious in terms of the time and energy you can free up to devote to this. Slow but steady progress is likely to be intrinsically motivating here and as this builds it should become self-sustaining. Success in working well with your peers will be enabled, and empowered in terms of its ultimate potential to impact the organization, by your relationships upwards with senior executives, which is where we now turn our attention.

Managing upwards

07

In this chapter we focus on managing upwards. We start by considering how to deal with difficult or dysfunctional relationships with more senior people, particularly if this is with your boss. We consider how broader negative toxic cultures can form and serve to increase the likelihood of problematic upwards relationships. We also highlight the importance of being an active and effective follower as a middle manager. Regardless of how negative or positive your relationships are upwards, you will still need to actively manage the demands that flow from above and we review the most important factors in doing so. The need to form a positive partnership with your senior manager is considered and we finish the chapter by discussing how a broader range of senior stakeholders can be successfully managed.

Your relationships upwards, particularly with your manager, will have an enormous impact on your wellbeing, motivation and performance. In Chapter 2 we considered what life at the most senior level in a business or organization is like. We touched on strategic and personal drivers and power dynamics. We build on that in this chapter by focusing in detail on the relationships between middle and senior managers and what you can do from the middle position to work well with those at the top.

Towards the end of the last chapter we discussed the importance of middle management activity in contrast to leadership activity. Both are important but we argue that management has been devalued in recent years. At the most senior level in organizations the emphasis tends to be very much on leading rather than managing. This provides an opportunity for the middle manager to complement the senior executive. Your boss is likely to be expected to show strategic and transformational leadership, as well as being actively encouraged not to get involved in too much detailed management activity. This leaves a gap that you can fill. If you can do this well and work with your manager you are likely to build a strong and effective partnership that is mutually satisfying and beneficial.

It is fundamentally important that you are clear on what kind of relationship you want with your boss. Do you want his job? Are you content to work for her for the long term? Your career motivations, short and longer term, will have an impact here. If you are striving to reach the top, you are likely to form a different relationship than if you are happy to stay at the level you have reached. This does not mean the former has to be a negative relationship but there may be a natural strain in it that the latter does not have. If your boss knows that ultimately you want to fill his or her shoes, he or she may occasionally be slightly more suspicious of your motives, although this need not always be the case.

We want to start here by considering dysfunctional or difficult relationships upwards, not because we are assuming they are a given, or even common, but because when they occur it is very difficult to operate effectively. Even if your existing relationship with your manager is very positive there is a reasonable chance that you will experience a difficult upwards relationship at some point in your career. We will gradually get onto more positive ground, considering how functional and effective relationships can be formed and continued with those at the most senior levels.

Difficult upwards relationships

A very useful research-based classification of difficult relationships upwards is provided by Rose *et al* (2015). They highlight two core dimensions: **function/dysfunction** – the broad impact of the boss's behaviour on work and overall effectiveness, and **annoyance/trauma** – the narrower impact on the individual exposed to the boss's behaviour.

It's quite useful to draw a distinction between your manager's impact on you and on the broader work and effectiveness. Most people in the workplace will experience some annoyance with their manager: it's part of a normal relationship. However, if this becomes extreme, sustained and traumatic then it should be tackled, regardless of its wider dysfunctional impact.

Hopefully, you never work for a bullying boss – but if you do and he or she is at the organization's most senior level it can be very difficult to challenge the behaviour. First, we need to be clear on what constitutes workplace bullying: it is 'by definition characterized by systematic and prolonged exposure to repeated negative and aggressive behaviour of a primarily psychological nature, including non-behaviour and acts of social exclusion' (Nielsen and Einarsen, 2012: 309). So a one-off act usually isn't really bullying. If your boss is having a very bad time and uncharacteristically shouts and swears at you, it's inappropriate and unprofessional behaviour that should be challenged. But bullying tends to be prolonged victimization, usually over an extended period.

The exclusion aspect of bullying is worth considering. Being deliberately excluded and isolated can be traumatic. Social isolation sits firmly in the traumatic side in the Rose *et al* classification. Canadian research shows that being isolated at work may be more harmful than being actively harassed (O'Reilly *et al,* 2014). The researchers found that being ostracized at work was generally considered by most people in organizations as being less harmful and more socially acceptable than being harassed. However, their research showed that the negative impact, particularly in terms of wellbeing and employee turnover, was more severe for those ostracized and isolated in comparison to those experiencing direct harassment. They also found that feeling ostracized was more common than feeling harassed.

In middle management being deliberately isolated by your boss can be particularly difficult. Of course having a strong peer network is likely to have buffering effect on this to some extent, at least in terms of your psychological wellbeing. The key to addressing this successfully in the long term is to consider potential causes. There are probably only a few possible reasons for being isolated by your boss. The first, and the most difficult to change, is that he or she feels personally threatened by you. Good leaders, we would argue, should look to develop people who work for them towards being better than they are themselves. While most leaders agree with this proposition at a rational level, not all manage it at an emotional one. This is where an open conversation about motives is essential. Clearly if ultimately you aspire to do your boss's job, and make little secret of this, you are going to have to reassure him or her that you are not a direct threat to his or her position! If your ambition is to replace your boss at all costs, then you can hardly be surprised if you meet with a high degree of defensive reaction. However, if this is not your core purpose then an open conversation with your manager may help to reduce defensiveness on his or her part. You should be prepared to be as open as possible in this discussion about your career aspirations and general motivators. If you do this, probably in more than one conversation, it should help make it less likely that your boss sees you as a threat, although that's obviously not a given.

Another reason that you can end up feeling isolated, and perhaps even ostracized, by your boss is that you just don't spend enough time talking to each other about the right stuff. By this we mean strategically important priorities and how you are progressing against them. Normally you can bring to this a more informed picture of how strategic goals are translating into activity than your senior manager will have. Senior managers should appreciate being updated, and it is likely to be reciprocated with more openness on their part regarding strategic direction. The key is to ensure these conversations happen regularly and that you don't fall into a pattern of the only exchanges being crisis-like specific task discussions. In our experience many middle, and indeed senior managers, feel they do not consistently devote enough time to truly strategic discussions.

If your boss is more explicitly bullying and intimidating, you need to find a way to challenge that behaviour. It is useful to understand what drives this, but your initial priority should be to challenge its unacceptability regardless of the root cause. The sooner you make the challenge the better. Tolerating intimidating or abusive behaviour only makes it increasingly difficult to take control and face the individual with your concerns. If you feel you can challenge your boss directly in this situation, that is probably the best first step. Make him or her aware that you consider aspects of his or her behaviour to be unfair and unacceptable to you. Be ready to cite specific examples. However, it is quite unlikely that managers will immediately accept that they are out of line and change their behaviour. You are likely to hear a number of excuses, the most prominent tending to be along the lines of these being tough times and they are under a lot of pressure and need to push hard for high performance. This tough manager stance can be difficult to counter, but there is a difference between tough but fair management and bullying. In the UK the CIPD (2005) publishes a useful guide that highlights some of the differences. Table 7.1 draws on this and illustrates three potential differences between legitimately strong senior managers who claim they need to challenge you hard to improve your performance, and a bully.

Table 7.1   Strong performance management and bullying

Legitimate strong performance management	Bullying
Looking at all the potential reasons for poor performance, eg people, systems, training and equipment.	No attempt being made to identify the nature or source of the poor performance.
Setting and agreeing standards of performance and behaviour consultatively.	Imposing new standards without any discussion on appropriate standards of performance or behaviour.
Recognizing and rewarding improvements in performance, attitudes and behaviours.	Rewards and recognition are arbitrary and acts of favouritism.

Taking these three together, bullying would be characterized by a senior manager assuming you were the only source of performance problems, who was not prepared to properly discuss and agree changes in requirements, and who did not fairly recognize and reward positive performance – sound familiar? In our experience this is unfortunately not as rare a profile as it should be.

A direct challenge to a bullying senior manager can be difficult. Even if you adopt this strategy it is useful to have a back-up plan. This may mean approaching another senior manager or executive with your concerns, perhaps even the chief executive if you are one level below the executive team. If you go down this route, and it may be the right choice, you will need to be clear and specific about the behaviour you believe constitutes bullying.

It is worth considering further why some senior managers and executives resort to inappropriate intimidating behaviour at times. Is it because at this level they have more personality flaws, perhaps even being more likely to have psychotic traits? There have been some suggestions in recent years that this may be the case (Boddy *et al*, 2010). So-called 'corporate psychopaths' are thought to be very rare but their negative interpersonal impact can be disproportionately large. For example, Boddy (2011) concluded that while corporate psychopaths account for only 1 per cent of the working population they are responsible for 26 per cent of bullying. If you believe you are being bullied by a senior executive with psychopathic tendencies, there is probably no point trying to reason with him or her about his or her behaviour. Psychopaths' lack of empathy and self-serving outlook mean it is extremely unlikely that they will respond constructively to your concerns and feedback. Nevertheless, you may not be able to tell that this is the case until you have tried challenging them directly.

Fortunately, such extreme negative personality types are rare, even at the top. In our experience it is much more likely that senior managers display intimidating or bullying behaviour as a result of a combination of not effectively handling the pressure they are under, and poorly developed people management skills. When this is the case there is reasonable scope for successfully challenging and changing their behaviour. A starting point for doing so is often to shock them by stating just how negative some of their behaviour can be in terms of its impact on you, and possibly others. It can help to be open about how their bullying behaviour makes you feel and the ways it affects your wellbeing. This might be an eye-opener for some, resulting in them seeking coaching or other support to address their triggers and interpersonal style under pressure.

Toxic leadership cultures

What if the negative interpersonal issues you experience with those at a more senior level go well beyond your direct line relationship? Assuming you have considered that you may be part of the problem and discounted this idea, it is possible that you are working in a culture permeated by toxic leadership at the most senior level. This state occurs when a toxic triangle is in place (Padilla *et al,* 2007). The triangle represents three conditions that in combination define a toxic working relationship: destructive leadership, susceptible followers (conformers, colluders) and conducive environments. This is useful as it does not just focus on the characteristics of senior leaders but emphasizes the interaction of leader qualities, follower susceptibility and environmental factors. The two types of susceptible followers identified are particularly worth considering here: conformers and colluders. Padilla and his colleagues define these:

> Conformers comply with destructive leaders out of fear whereas colluders actively participate in the destructive leader's agenda. Both types are motivated by self-interest but their concerns are different: conformers try to minimize the consequences of not going along, while colluders seek personal gain through association with a destructive leader. (Padilla *et al,* 2007: 183)

So a healthy culture is one where there are few destructive leaders at the top and there aren't too many conformers or colluders at middle management level. If the opposite is true, and the wider environment is unstable and vulnerable, then we have the conditions for a toxic triangle.

Being a good follower

The emphasis on followership is important for middle managers. Much has been written about leadership but much less about followership, yet in many ways leadership is best defined by having followers. In fact, if you don't have any followers you can hardly credibly call yourself a leader! As a middle manager you need to be an effective follower, as well as an effective leader. While leading is what seems to get most kudos, we may underestimate the importance of following at our peril:

> Followership may take the backseat to leadership but it matters: it matters a lot!... At the extreme, weak leadership and weak followership are two sides of the same coin and the consequence is always the same: organizational confusion and poor performance. (McCallum, 2013)

As a middle manager, what does being an effective follower mean in practice? Clearly being either a complete conformer or colluder is not ideal. Robert Kelley (2008), who was responsible for bringing the idea of followership into the business mainstream with his 1988 classic *HBR* article 'In praise of followers', identifies five basic styles of followership:

- *The Sheep*: passive, look to their leader to do their thinking for them without having to figure out what is going on for themselves.

- *The Yes-people*: positive, always on the leader's side, but also passive in terms of independent thinking and action.

- *The Alienated*: think for themselves, but tend to be sceptical or cynical. Often see themselves independent from organizational norms, the only people who have the courage to call it as it is and stand up to the boss when necessary.

- *The Pragmatics*: sit on the fence and observe how change pans out before committing themselves. They tend to see themselves maintaining the traditional ways of doing things. Their attitude tends to be that leaders and new strategies come and go, and if they just keep doing what they normally do, they will survive waves of change.

- *The Star Followers*: think for themselves, are very active with positive energy. They do not accept the leader's decision without evaluating it. If they agree with the leader, they give full commitment and support. When they disagree, they challenge, seeking to provide constructive alternatives.

Just as situational leadership holds true, there may be a case for situational followership. There could be times when adopting 'yes-people' behaviour is the right response facing a dominant senior manager, or reserving your judgement like a 'pragmatic'. However, in the main the 'star follower' should be the most consistently effective followership mode to adopt as a middle manager. This is a role that is actually a form of servant leadership. Playing this role, you serve your manager well – by helping him or her refine and improve his or her thinking and activity. You serve those that work for you well by actively seeking to collaborate upwards to ensure the best strategy is implemented. You also serve yourself by taking control in an active way, feeling that you are making a shaping contribution to direction.

Adopting a mature servant mode does not mean subservience. You will serve the senior leadership of the organization well through constructive challenge rather than unquestioning compliant support. There is something inherently psychologically healthy in this state. It avoids self-absorption and victim-like attitudes. However, it is not something you can just decide to use as a tactical approach: it needs to come from deeper. It is dependent upon a values alignment, and belief in the capability of senior managers. When your personal values are a close fit with those of the organization you work for, and you believe senior management truly share these values, there is a strong basis for a servant orientation. This state produces an outward-looking sense of purpose, and this combination can maximize contentment, wellbeing and sustainably high levels of performance.

Managing demands from above

You may not have to suffer a bullying or toxic senior manager. However, you will almost certainly need to have strategies to actively manage the demands and expectation that come from the top. In some senses the more successful you have been in the past the more likely you are to meet increasing demands from the top in the future. The absolute key to managing these is goal clarity regarding your role and business objectives. You need to be clear about how you truly add value to your business or organization in your role. This should be articulated and agreed with your manager. The starting point for doing this well is to properly understand, and then be able to articulate, the core value you add. Key questions to ask yourself that can help to clarify this include:

- How do I add value to what my boss needs to achieve?
- Where do my team most need me to contribute to add value to our collective goals?
- Where do I add most value to my peers in other functions?
- Can I measure the value I add?

The last of these questions is usually particularly challenging, but it is a useful one to try to answer. Not all of the value you add will be tangible or quantifiable. In fact, depending on your role, most of your value add may be qualitative and intangible. For example, if you are responsible for leadership development or culture change, and you are effective, you will almost certainly add a lot of intangible value to your business or organization. This doesn't mean it's not real – but it does need to be articulated and agreed. This will be important in any middle management role. Say some team members ask you to meet them to discuss an important problem they are trying to solve and you help them to move forward with it; how can that value add be captured? If it can't, does this mean it shouldn't be a priority? This places an emphasis on clarity and agreement with your boss on the nature of the range of value you add. Without such discussions there is a high risk of frequent disagreement over priorities. A balanced scorecard type approach can be helpful here.

The balanced scorecard was developed by Kaplan and Norton (1992) as a strategic management tool. It considers the range of drivers and measures of value, both hard (eg profit) and soft (eg organizational learning). It is split into four perspectives:

1 financial performance (eg sales, profit);

2 internal business (process) perspective;

3 innovation and learning; and

4 customer perspective.

Table 7.2 suggests some performance indicators that are likely to be relevant for a middle manager. Obviously the specific indicators that apply will be function/role dependent.

Table 7.2 Middle manager balanced scorecard indicators

Perspective	Potential middle manager indicators
Financial performance	Sales attribution, divisional/departmental turnover and profit, revenue per customer or client.
Internal business	Strategy implementation process efficiency, upwards and downwards communication flow, cross-departmental communication mechanisms, business reporting efficiency.
Innovation and learning	New products or services developed from changes in strategic direction. Peer mentoring contribution.
Customer perspective	Customer satisfaction ratings. Internal customer feedback. Customer retention.

Agreeing a scorecard with your manager will help to share and clarify goals and expectations. It is a tangible source of reference that you can come back to regularly when discussing priorities and workload. This can be particularly important when facing a period of major change that needs to be managed in consultation with your boss (Marin, 2012). As with many such techniques, its main value is in the structured and focused conversations that it can support.

With clarity about value add you are in a position to properly prioritize, and have a strong foundation from which to push back when your boss makes unreasonable demands. This is particularly important if you have a manager who likes to work in constant crisis management mode, which some leaders seem to relish. If your boss says, 'I am at my best in a crisis' watch out for him or her stimulating a crisis to be at their best! Your manager may be like this because he or she is hooked on the stress hormones that flow when in this state, such as adrenalin and cortisol. Or, he or she may just be very disorganized and as a result leave too many things to the last minute. To be able to avoid getting sucked into this constant state of firefighting you need a well-developed sense of what is truly important and urgent and what isn't. This enables you to provide a strong argument, when you need to, that the response your boss demands isn't necessarily the right one.

If you work for a pathologically disorganized manager you can supply support by helping him or her to stay better organized for the most strategically important activity. You don't need to become a PA, and shouldn't try to fill an admin role. It is more about working with managers to ensure you stay as planned and organized as possible about what you agree are the strategic priorities. How you do this to best effect depends on a number of contextual factors, such as how closely you work with each other and your respective communication style preferences. However, one way may be to have a 'start the week' conversation about strategic priorities, and the key activities linked to them that you agree you need to spend time on and resource adequately. If new, genuinely important demands emerge then you are in a better position to understand how they fit strategically and the impact on other planned activity of responding to them.

Ultimately, as a middle manager in a large organization you are going to have too much to do most of the time. Accepting this is important for your wellbeing. Some managers we work with find this extremely difficult to do. This is often as a result of essentially a positive quality: a high level of drive manifesting in a desire to get everything done before you believe you are performing at your best. Breaking the psychological link between 'more' and 'best' is the critical point here. Consider this thought: you may be a more effective middle manager if you do less than you usually do. For some this is almost a pain-inducing thought. If you pride yourself on being someone who keeps working until the job is done, you could be in this category. The argument for doing less is that you will spend more time reflecting and focusing on what is truly most important. As a result, you will engage in activity that has a greater impact on your key goals and objectives. Another reason for doing less is to create and protect sufficient time to work reflectively and strategically with your boss.

Living with the fact that you may never get to the bottom of your in-tray is a lot easier if you feel you are getting through the most important stuff. If you believe your days, weeks and months are dominated by randomly responding to other people's priorities, including those from above, you are unlikely to be comfortable with the fact that there is always more that needs to be done. Clearly your boss isn't the only source of your overload, but the demands he or she places on you are probably the most acutely experienced. This will be compounded if you have a fractious or difficult relationship, or if your boss's style is crisis-driven.

Providing positive reinforcement upwards

You can serve your boss well by being a source of positive reinforcement. This isn't about butt kissing or cringing ingratiation, even though, as we mentioned previously, ingratiation can work on occasion. It's about contributing to a positive and genuine working relationship. Thanking your manager occasionally when you believe he or she has done something really effective or has been particularly supportive to you is the right thing to do, not least because it is part of a mature and respectful human relationship. If you Google 'thanking your boss' you will see a range of suggested greeting cards you should buy – as if this is a very rare special occasion that needs to be marked. If this is indeed an unusual occurrence, and it's not something you have done much of in the past, your boss's initial reaction may be scepticism, and he or she may wonder what lies behind your sudden show of gratitude. However, if you do this from time to time as part of your normal working relationship it will have a number of benefits.

It is likely that in most organizations we don't show gratitude towards more senior people nearly as much as we do sideways or downwards. This can leave people at the top with very little feedback from below on what they are doing right. As a result, they may not continue to do some activities that actually have really positive outcomes and add significant value. Infrequent positive reinforcement is a very powerful way of maintaining behaviour. It is more effective than providing no positive reinforcement, or overdoing it and saying everything the person does is wonderful. This will work with your boss just as well as it does with anyone else. So if you genuinely rate or value some of the things your manager does, it's worth saying thank you every now and again and saying why you think what he or she has done makes a positive difference.

In Chapter 1 we mentioned the work of Fredrickson and her colleagues and their 'broaden and build' theory on positive emotions. This is relevant here. If you never provide any upwards positive feedback to your boss, you can develop a negative emotional bias in your relationship. This then makes it less likely you will be genuinely open with each other and collaborate in a way that helps you to be broad and innovative in how you deal with issues and resolve problems. Receiving occasional positive feedback boosts the extent to which we feel valued and opens us up to thinking about what more we could do, rather than what we shouldn't be doing. In an interaction with your boss this could lead to him or her thinking, possibly subconsciously, about what else he or she could do that would please you. However, this does not mean that this should be your primary motive for providing the positive feedback. If it is, your manager will probably pick this up and the interaction won't be natural and authentic.

Developing a true partnership with your boss

Essentially, working well with a boss who is at or very close to the most senior level in the organization needs a partnership approach. It requires, in transactional analysis terms, an adult-adult relationship and not a parent-child one. The latter is characterized by emotional dependency and deference, the former by maturity, rationality and mutual respect. This doesn't mean that emotions are unimportant in adult-adult mode – emotions are always important. But this is a state where people engage in an emotionally mature way, managing their feelings and reactions, and as a result can usually be rational and solve problems through an open and honest exchange.

As a middle manager the partnership you can form with a good boss will effectively be one that provides a strong management-leadership coalition that can have a major impact across your organization. To illustrate this, consider how leadership practices could be enhanced through such an effective partnership. Kouzes and Posner (2007) argue compellingly for five key leadership practices. These are listed below with suggestions for how they can be enhanced through a strong middle-senior manager partnership:

1 *Model the way* – walking the talk and demonstrating through behaviour the way for others to follow. In partnership with a senior manager you can provide a consistent and credible model of

how to operate for others to follow. A strong alignment between middle and senior management in terms of key behaviours provides a powerful leadership model for most levels in the hierarchy to note and follow.

2 *Inspire a shared vision* – ensuring you have a genuinely shared vision of where the business or organization is heading helps middle and senior managers to prioritize and collaborate more and provides clarity of direction for others.

3 *Challenge the process* – an open, healthy relationship between the middle and the top allows processes to be challenged from multiple perspectives. It also normalizes constructive challenge and sends a signal to others that this is not only the right thing to do but is expected.

4 *Enable others to act* – you start by enabling each other to act to your full potential. You can then work together to ensure others are suitably and truly empowered and enabled.

5 *Encourage the heart* – collectively you can set the tone for the organization, recognizing that we are all human and have emotional as well as rational needs. Meeting these needs and tuning into emotional drivers can unlock potential. It also maximizes positive emotional experience, which can produce a virtuous spiral in terms of wellbeing, innovation and performance improvement.

Any middle or senior manager can lead effectively by addressing the above practices independently. However, by working together across them they can have a much broader and more sustained impact.

In a sense when you work in partnership with someone at the top you combine the best of leadership and management. It's not as simple as saying the people at the top lead and middle managers manage. However, on balance the latter should manage more than they lead and the former lead more than they manage. If you can harness the best of both in a strong partnership with your senior manager or executive, you have a formidable base for delivering high performance.

In seeking to develop a strong partnership relationship with your boss it may also be useful to get to know them at a personal level. This does not need to mean that you try to make them your best friend. However, recognizing that they have a life beyond your transactional workplace relationship, and taking some interest in this, can help the relationship. It is also an approach that is likely to be welcomed and reciprocated.

Managing a range of senior stakeholders

To be outstanding in the middle you need to consider a range of senior stakeholders, not just manage your relationship with your own boss. Research has shown (Englund and Bocero, 2006), that the active support of stakeholders from the senior leadership team is a critical factor in creating success. Effective middle managers understand this and are also willing to do whatever is necessary to ensure that their senior stakeholders understand and fulfil their role (Cooke-Davies, 2005).

So, what is your strategy for managing your senior stakeholders? Depending on your level and the size and complexity of your organization, this could be a large number of people or a relatively small group. It does not need to be everyone at a more senior level. First of all, you need to decide if different senior individuals really are a stakeholder in what you do. Do they have any sort of influence over what you are trying to achieve? Do you need their support to reach your objectives? Should they legitimately be consulted about some of the work you do? When you have decided who your senior stakeholders are, you should map the nature of your relationship with them. The extent to which you structure this will be mainly dependent on the number of senior stakeholders you have, as well as the complexity of your organizational structure. Your own working style will also have an impact on how detailed an approach you prefer.

The nature of power relationships at a senior level, which we introduced in Chapter 2, is very relevant here. Obviously your direct line manager is the main power lens that you most need to be able to see through. However, the nature of how power plays out more broadly at a senior level is likely to regularly impact your working environment. If there is obvious conflict there, you need to understand its impact on you and think about how you can either actively manage this or at least ensure you do what you can to reduce the risk that it may significantly derail you.

Ultimately you may decide that there are only a few people at senior level that you need to actively stakeholder manage. If that is the case, you are unlikely to need to use a formal stakeholder mapping approach. However, the principles apply, and it is certainly worth taking this perspective from time to time. Sophisticated approaches are powerful and can reveal important nuances and influences, particularly those that help you to visualize your senior stakeholder landscape (Bourne and Walker, 2005). At the core of stakeholder mapping is the need to identify mutual interactivity and power. It is important to consider both of these aspects. For example, a senior stakeholder may interact frequently with you on some aspect of the resources you have available but have limited power to increase or reduce them. Alternatively, another senior executive may not interact with you frequently but have a lot of power to influence your available resource levels, if they choose to exercise it at any point. Your strategy for dealing with these stakeholders will be different, but both merit having one.

From managing at work to managing your lifestyle

In the last three chapters we have focused on managing relationships at work – with your team, your same-level peers, and upwards. This will be a lot easier if you maintain a healthy and productive lifestyle generally. This is where we turn our attention in the next chapter. The need for a whole-person approach to being an outstanding middle manager is fundamentally important. The interaction between your lifestyle generally and how effective and happy you are at work is reciprocal and critically important. Your overall lifestyle will also have an impact on your motivation at work and your career.

Lifestyle management

08

In this chapter we take a whole-person approach and consider the importance of lifestyle management to sustainable success and happiness as a middle manager. We highlight evidence relating to the interplay between work and broader life factors. We then go on to discuss key lifestyle factors: exercise, food and fuel, and sleep. We consider relationship issues and review the role that mindfulness can play in improving health and effectiveness.

It is likely that you are reading this book with your main focus being the reality of middle management in the workplace. You may not have expected to see a chapter on lifestyle management. However, as we said in Chapter 1, we believe you can only be effective in the long term by taking a whole-person approach. To be outstanding in mid-level roles in a sustainable way you need to actively manage your whole lifestyle. If you think your life away from work doesn't have an impact on your work motivation, wellbeing and performance, you are kidding yourself. Equally, if you believe that the pressures you experience when working have no impact on the rest of your life, we will seek to challenge your view in this chapter.

The impact of work on life and life on work

So what impact does your wellbeing at work have on the rest of your life, and what's the impact of being well and happy outside of work on your working life? First of all, there is plenty of evidence that good work has a positive impact on your general health and wellbeing (Waddell and Burton, 2006). In the UK the think tank The Work Foundation has been particularly active in recent years in emphasizing the importance of 'good work' for our overall health and wellbeing, as well as for business performance and productivity. It produced a number of research and policy guidance documents seeking to make the case for good work and particularly its impact on health. Its ethos is summarized as follows:

> Recent studies have shown that 'bad work' is even worse for physical and mental health than unemployment... good work is productive and efficient, aims to involve and engage employees and to encourage their contribution to organizational success. (The Work Foundation, 2016)

Clearly there are social values embedded within this statement, but this vision of good work and its impact is supported by a growing evidence base. Bevan (2012), drawing on the work of Coats (2006), highlights the following core elements of good work:

- Secure and interesting jobs that employees find fulfilling, which contribute to the achievement of high performance and sustainable business success.
- A style and ethos of management that is based on high levels of trust and recognizes that managing people fairly and effectively is crucial to skilled work and high performance.
- Choice, flexibility and control over working hours.
- Autonomy and control over the pace of work and the working environment.
- Voice for employees in the critical employer decisions that affect their futures.

So what would that look like for a middle manager? Probably something like this:

- A fulfilling role where you believe you are making a positive impact in all directions.
- Trust-based open relationships with senior management, your team and same-level peers.
- Flexibility on when and where you work.
- The authority to make important decisions about the nature and flow of work for you and your team, without constant referral upwards.
- Being listened to and consulted by the executive team.

If this defines your work and role it will almost certainly have a positive impact on the rest of your life. If none, or very little, of this feels true for you it will probably have an even larger negative impact on your whole life experience.

A key determinant of the extent to which work pressures have an impact on the rest of your life is the perceived intensity of work. Work intensity is independent of working hours. There is evidence that many people feel they increasingly need to work very hard and intensely throughout their working day (CIPD, 2014). The impact of this is primarily exhaustion. You may be capable of very hard work throughout your working week, you probably enjoy large parts of this, but it can still leave you physically and psychologically exhausted. Very intense work is also difficult to switch off from. It can be difficult to get sufficient respite before you throw yourself back into the next phase of high intensity working. The risk is that we end up going through regular cycles of intensity and exhaustion. This is unlikely to feel balanced, and may turn what is intrinsically good work into feeling like bad work. Recognizing that breaking the intensity-exhaustion cycle may help you to enjoy and get more from the work that you do is key. However, it's a difficult cycle to disrupt when you are experiencing it – you are either too busy to do so or too tired.

The impact of good work can be very positive on life outside of work, particularly on relationships with family. In fact, when work is having a positive impact on our family life it tends to increase our job satisfaction (Carlson *et al*, 2011): a good reason for employers to do what they can to reduce the risks of work adversely affecting employees' family life.

So there is a definite impact of work, good or bad, on broader life. This seems to be particularly clear with the impact on family life. There is also evidence of an impact in the other direction. One interesting area, particularly for middle managers, is the impact of family life on decision making at work. In the main this is most relevant when it comes to major work decisions such as whether to accept an overseas posting, or to apply for a new role or position. Greenhaus and Powell (2012) bring in the notion of the family-relatedness of work decisions. This could be very relevant for mid-level people at key points both in terms of the choices they make for themselves and the decisions they make about others, such as members of their team. Recognizing that there are times when family circumstances are likely to affect work decisions for you and others is important, and the sensible response is to ensure the pertinent factors can be properly aired and considered.

In reality the pressures and pleasures you experience at work and in the rest of your life interact in terms of the impact they have on you. How engaged you are in your work and organization is an important factor to consider alongside your overall work-life balance. A useful framework that helps to understand this was produced from research commissioned by the Bank Workers Charity in the UK. Based on well-being survey data from UK bank workers the research highlights four broad psychological and behavioural responses (see Table 8.1).

There are a few interesting findings here in relation to the interplay between work and the rest of your life. The daily hassles referred to were life stressors that can have a cumulative and knock-on effect, such as poor sleep quality, financial worries and the weather! Note that the most positive group, the Career optimizers (good work-life balance and high engagement) experience fewest daily hassles. This group are the most likely to use flexible working and the majority stick to their contracted hours. Separating cause and effect here is very difficult, but that's because causation is probably bi-directional and cyclical. So if you work flexibly, and generally stick close to your

Table 8.1 The interaction of work-life balance concerns and engagement (based on Bank Workers Charity, 2013)

Career optimizers (23% of sample)	High engagement	Fire fighters (24% of sample)
Key demographics: 43% aged over 40 34% with caring responsibilities 61% use flexible working 53% tenure 10 years+ 53% working contracted hours		*Key demographics:* 56% aged over 40 41% with caring responsibilities 59% use flexible working 62% tenure 10 years+ 15% working contracted hours
Average number of daily hassles: 7 Self-reported productivity: 85%		Average number of daily hassles: 10 Self-reported productivity: 85%
Good work-life balance	*UK Bank Workers*	**Troubling work-life balance**
Untapped potential (20% of sample)	Low engagement	**Captives** (27% of sample)
Key demographics: 57% aged over 40 29% with caring responsibilities 50% use flexible working 58% tenure 10 years+ 65% working contracted hours		*Key demographics:* 65% aged over 40 35% with caring responsibilities 52% use flexible working 60% tenure 10 years+ 18% working contracted hours
Average number of daily hassles: 11 Self-reported productivity: 71%		Average number of daily hassles: 12 Self-reported productivity: 70%

contracted hours, it presumably gives you more time and space to deal with non-work hassles and as a result they attenuate in terms of their impact. Of course, this is the youngest of the four groups so perhaps they have yet to experience the full pressure of middle management. Note that this is a very productive group, but in contrast with the Fire fighters group, this productivity does not seem to be at the expense of a reasonable work-life balance. Fire fighters see themselves as being very productive, but at the cost of feeling they have a good work-life balance. This is a high burn-out risk category, particularly when you consider they have the highest level of caring responsibilities. If this category best describes you there is an increased health risk and your relationships outside of work may well be regularly compromised.

Obviously the place you definitely don't want to end up in middle management is the Captive category. This group has both low engagement and poor work-life balance. This is a long-service group who experience dissatisfaction in their working lives and relatively high stressors away from work. If you believe this fits your experience, we hope this book provides some inspiration and strategies for addressing your situation.

The Untapped potential group may be more relevant in terms of it fitting the experience of some people who work in your team. These are people who aren't too worried about their work-life balance, but their meaning or purpose relating to work has probably long gone. They are a rust-out rather than burn-out risk group. They need to be re-engaged and motivated but in a way that does not necessarily adversely impact their work-life balance. This is often about getting them involved in different work activities rather than more. Their working experience needs refreshing: they need different work, not more of it.

To some degree drawing a firm distinction between work and the rest of our life is artificial, not least because the line between the two is often blurred. For many middle managers it makes more sense to think of work as an activity rather than a place. In recent years, the notion that work-life integration is a more useful concept than work-life balance has grown. The argument is that rather than thinking of work and life as opposing forces pulling you in different directions, it is more helpful to consider how work is integrated into the rest of your life. In many ways this seems sensible and, given the increasingly diffuse boundaries between the two domains, probably more accurate. However, individual differences are very important here.

The extent to which people are comfortable with a blurred distinction between work and the rest of their life is likely to depend on personality, values and career orientation. Some people clearly prefer to keep a solid boundary between work and the rest of their life. One argument for doing so is to reduce the risks of overworking and of never switching off properly from work to ensure sufficient respite periods. Without a firm work/non-work time/place distinction these risks can be very real. In Chapter 4 we discussed the importance of understanding your career anchors. It is possible that a preference for different anchors has an impact on how comfortable you are with a diffuse work-life boundary.

However, the most important career orientation here is having a protean one. Direnzo *et al* (2015: 538) define a protean career orientation as essentially autonomous career management and highlight two core components:

(1) a self-directed approach to career management in which the individual exerts personal control over career development by taking the initiative to explore career options and make career decisions; (2) a values-driven orientation whereby the individual pursues personally meaningful (as opposed to socially imposed) values and goals that provide the motivation behind career decisions and create the standards for experiencing psychological career success.

These researchers found a positive relationship between having a protean career orientation (PCO) and work-life balance. Crucially they also found a strong relationship between having a PCO and adopting a whole-life perspective. They characterized the latter as taking decisions based on seeking satisfaction in multiple life roles, not just work. So our contention is that middle managers who take control of their own career, and seek meaning and purpose in many areas of their life, will experience a better balance and higher job and life satisfaction. It is so easy when immersed in the pressure of work in mid-level roles to start to feel you have no control over your direction or development and to lose sight of the fact that you may be neglecting other areas of your life that matter to you. There is a link here to psychological resilience, a concept we drew on heavily in Chapter 3. A whole-life perspective is a core source of resilience. It reduces the risk of losing perspective and of work-caused burn-out.

If you are the kind of person who prefers to keep work and the rest of your life separate as much as possible you probably need a buffer between the two. This is activity that helps you make the transition between the two domains. It might be physical exercise, listening to music, or a specific mental relaxation exercise. In the main this is likely to be most needed to move from work to home mode, rather than the other way round. Perhaps there is an argument for a routine that helps you fully engage in work mode, but most people tend to value the end-of-work buffer most. If on the other hand you do not mind mingling work and the rest of your life, a buffer between the two is not usually required.

If you are content with a weak or non-existent boundary between work and the rest of your life there are still two challenges we'd pose. Is there a personal cost to operating in this way? Is there a negative impact on your partner or family? You may love your work and see it as a natural part of your life without the need to keep it in any particular compartment. However, working too long, even at something you love, can have detrimental effects. We all need respite for health and performance reasons. In addition, proper periods of disconnection can help you come back to work refreshed and help you take a new perspective on difficult problems and issues.

It needs an understanding partner and family to cope with someone who is not clear on when they are working and when they are not. Perhaps the key to this is transparency and involvement. If you open up to your family about what your work entails and what it means to you it should help them to appreciate what you are doing and why. Of course this could also lead them to the conclusion that your work doesn't always merit taking as much of your time and attention as it does!

If you live with a partner who also works full-time then work-life balance can be particularly challenging. If you both have caring responsibilities, the challenge is further magnified. Neal and Hammer

(2009) reviewed work-life coping strategies for dual-career couples (all heterosexual) with sandwich generation caring responsibilities (for both children and elderly parents). A couple of particularly interesting findings emerged: 1) for women, coping strategies that bolster emotional resources were associated with lower levels of depression and experiencing a more positive interplay between work and life; and 2) for both men and women, emotional and prioritization coping strategies had a significant impact on wellbeing, while those that decreased social involvement had a negative impact.

Emotional coping strategies are where people openly and freely express their emotions without necessarily seeking to analyse them or find their rational cause. The emotional release can be enough, sometimes. Prioritization strategies on the other hand are more rational/logical and help individuals feel better by working at getting on top of their pressures and finding a structure and priority order for dealing with them.

In general, the risk is that the more stretched you are in trying to balance multiple work and family responsibilities, and probably as a result withdraw from a wider social circle, the more detrimental it is to your wellbeing. This is a completely understandable spiral and probably a very difficult one to break. If you are in this position it therefore becomes important to use whatever coping mechanisms you can in terms of emotional support and prioritizing your commitments.

It is clear that work and life away from work impact each other. If you strive to be outstanding in your middle management role, with the organizational squeeze pressures that this brings, you will need to take a whole-person approach. This means ensuring you do all you can to maintain your health and wellbeing. We now review the lifestyle factors that are most important in doing so.

Maintaining your health and wellbeing

Exercise – keeping fit for life

The benefits of regular exercise for your health are well established. In terms of your mental state, how regularly you exercise is probably one of the best predictors of psychological wellbeing (Penedo and Dahn, 2005). Of course the challenge is not knowing this: it's doing it consistently. One model that is particularly helpful here is the Health Action Process Approach (Schwarzer, 2008). This demonstrates how motivational (eg self-efficacy) and volitional (eg action planning) aspects interact to produce healthy or unhealthy behaviours and habits. Applying this to striving to increase the amount of regular exercise suggests the following aspects are particularly important:

- generally visioning success (goal) rather than failure;
- positive outcome expectancy (eg 'If I exercise five times a week, I will reduce my cardiovascular risk');
- optimistic beliefs about capability to deal with barriers;
- action planning: when, where, how;
- planning alternatives (eg 'I plan to run on Sunday but if the weather is lousy, I will go to the gym instead');
- trusting your ability to regain control after a setback or failure.

As a busy middle manager it is very likely that there will be times when you feel you have far too much to do to take time out to exercise. Essentially you need to recognize that this is a conscious choice and to carefully consider whether it is the right one to make, particularly if you do so frequently. There is always more to do, but you will be in a much better state to do it if you regularly exercise.

You tend to know you are in the right place when you exercise habitually: it's just something you do regularly as a natural part of your life, like cleaning your teeth. A habit is something you do without being too aware of what you are doing. When trying to develop a new exercise habit you need to learn how to manage your self-talk or inner chimp (Peters, 2012). If you listen to this too much you will mostly talk yourself out of taking exercise. This will seem very rational at the time that this inner conversation is taking place, for example:

> It's a nice morning, perhaps I should cycle to work. Yes, that will do me good, I'll do that. I'll need to leave half an hour earlier though to give myself time to shower and change when I get there. I've got a meeting

first thing, I don't want to arrive looking sweaty. On second thoughts
I'll leave it until tomorrow... (repeat a variation of this the next day).

This kind of self-talk is to an extent inevitable. The breakthrough
comes when you can let it play out but continue to do what you
should – take the exercise. One strategy that clearly doesn't work
well with exercise is to wait until you feel like it. If you are tired you
are much more likely to reach for an alternative coping resource, perhaps one that comes in packets or bottles, than to take exercise.
Relying solely on willpower usually isn't a great strategy. Finding an
activity you really enjoy and then truly building it into your life
are key. Perhaps you don't join the gym in January like everyone else?
If you can integrate exercise into your regular day (eg cycling to work
as your default form of transport) then it has more chance of becoming habitual. Some find they can create and sustain more exercise
through a combination of goal setting and determination. For others
a social strategy can work better, such as joining an exercise class
with friends, and using peer pressure as a motivator. Whatever works
for you in the long term, the benefits you will gain from regular exercise will eventually become the strongest motivator for continuing to
undertake it.

Food and fuel

Garbage in, garbage out. It is so easy as we charge through busy lives
to eat and drink what is easily available and instantly satisfying.
Obesity levels in the Western world, and in many cases elsewhere,
continue to rise to the point of being understandably described as an
epidemic (Malik *et al*, 2013). Fast food chains have a uniform pres-
ence across the world. We may be smoking a lot less but our use of
other comforting substances, particularly alcohol, shows little sign of
abating.

The busier we are at work and in the rest of our lives, the less we
are likely to plan our eating and drinking. This is probably particularly true when it comes to workday lunch. One phenomenon we
have observed that won't help is the gradual disappearance of the
lunch break. Grabbing a sandwich and eating it at your desk while

continuing to work seems to be the norm for many people now. Leaving aside the detrimental psychological and social impact of this, it may well contribute to unhealthy eating. When you stop taking the time to choose your lunch and eat it at a leisurely pace you may go for instant gratification at the expense of healthy sustenance. You may counter this by preparing a healthy lunch at home and taking it in. However, this keep-going, eat-fast habit is worth challenging. If you do this as a manager you set an expectation, deliberately or not, that your team members should do the same.

Caffeine-fuelled days may be your norm. This drug in moderation seems to have a number of positive benefits but when you can't operate without it you may have a problem. Even if this is not damaging your health, which is debatable, it could be symptomatic of a general lack of lifestyle balance. Setting ourselves goals of perfection is probably setting ourselves up for failure. There will be times when you drink too much alcohol or eat the wrong food; it's ensuring this isn't your de facto lifestyle coping choice that is important. Breaking these unhealthy cycles effectively may be best achieved with small changes initially. For example, rather than just drinking coffee, make sure you always alternate with a glass of water. Just turning small changes into new habits can be the key to a more balanced fuelling of body and mind.

Sleep

In the last decade there has been a significant increase in research on sleep, much of this on the impact of sleep deprivation. This is providing a compelling and sophisticated evidence base for the negative impact of insufficient sleep on work performance, particularly in terms of cognition and decision making (Jackson *et al*, 2013). Sustained and chronic sleep deprivation also has a negative impact on health (Buysse, 2014; Luyster *et al*, 2012). There are many reasons for not getting enough sleep, or consistently poor quality sleep. Of course there are natural life stages, particularly with very young children, where there are limits over how much we can control this. However, this is another lifestyle area where we can often take action but either don't really try to, or tell ourselves it's beyond our control. Have you ever used, or heard others use justifications like:

- I'm just not a good sleeper.
- I can't switch off.
- I can survive very well on six hours sleep a night.
- I like to work late at night/very early in the morning, when there are no disruptions.
- I always seem to get drawn into late night television.

The first of these is a self-fulfilling attribution. It attributes the cause of not sleeping internally (as opposed to considering external environmental factors) and it's permanent and global (presumably the individual is not a good sleeper wherever and whenever he or she tries to sleep). This means you keep this close to you as a constant causal explanation for why you can't sleep and, not surprisingly it becomes self-fulfilling.

The second reason, not being able to switch off, may well be true some of the time. A key challenge here is whether you give yourself the opportunity to switch off before you try to sleep. If you are working late and then go straight to bed you can hardly be surprised if your head is swirling with thoughts about what you have just been concentrating on. This will be compounded if you are still working on your tablet or phone in bed before trying to sleep! A relaxation activity before sleeping is normally a good idea. There is also a possibility here of another self-fulfilling prediction. Believing you can't switch off may well prime your brain to not switch off!

Many people need more sleep than they think they do. There is a difference between being able to function and being able to function at your best. This may be linked to working late in the evening or very early in the morning to concentrate without distractions. Perhaps you'd be able to concentrate better with normal day-to-day distractions if you were consistently getting more sleep? A classic behavioural trap is that when you do finally slump in front of the TV after a long hard day, you end up watching whatever is on longer than you intended and lose sleep. This could be because you are using this as a mind drug to help you disconnect from the activity of the day. However, if you find something really interesting you should record it and try to stay disciplined about the time you go to bed, particularly during the working week.

There is plenty of good guidance on improving your sleep regime but the key is to recognize that, as with exercise and diet, we can end up in lifecycles and patterns that become self-perpetuating. Negative cycles feed themselves: things aren't going well at work, you are making the wrong choices for your health, and you have too many demands away from work. So do positive cycles: when we are feeling good about work it has a spill over into our home life and we are likely to make better health choices. The key is recognizing when you are slipping into a negative cycle and taking some action to break it. This is in addition to habitually undertaking activities likely to maintain positive cycles.

Fredrickson's 3:1 positivity ratio, which we mentioned in Chapter 5, is a good guide here (Fredrickson, 2009). She argues that aiming for three positive experiences for each negative one in life seems to be important. Whether the ratio turns out to be that precise is open to question and has been challenged (Brown *et al*, 2013). However, the idea that we need to create and nurture positive experiences with the goal of them outweighing negative ones seems sensible. This is probably best achieved through a combination of situational engineering and attitude change. It is not always possible to create inherently positive situations. Clearly there will be times in life when lots of things go wrong and it is superficial, unrealistic, and possibly damaging to just tell people to always look on the bright side. Psychologically, there is no light without shade. Nevertheless, there are usually things we can do to increase the likelihood of positive experiences at work and in the rest of your life. It is equally true that our attitude has an impact on whether ambiguous events are interpreted as positive or negative. When you are in a generally positive place in your life you tend to make better choices for your wellbeing and it has a knock-on impact on your work performance. Of course not everything goes well when you are in this space but you react better to setbacks and are less likely to be dragged into prolonged periods of negativity.

Relationships

If there is one aspect of your life you would regret neglecting due to work pressures more than any other, it is your relationships with your family and close friends. The importance of being able to spend regular high quality time with those that matter most to you can never be over-stated. Being at your best as a middle manager is significantly helped when you have happy and strong relationships at home. Ensuring you can be fully present for your family rather than constantly distracted by thoughts of work, or actual work, is important. Do you sit down with your family and are you all looking at your smartphones? Can you listen properly to your partner without worrying about what you are going to have to do at work tomorrow? Spending quality time with your close family will bring its own rewards, for them and for you, and is also likely to enhance your work relationships and experience. The two domains can enrich each other, for example: 'I think being a mother and having patience and watching someone else grow has made me a better manager. I am better able to be patient with other people and let them grow and develop in a way that is good for them.' (Ruderman *et al*, 2002, quoted in Greenhaus and Powell, 2006: 73)

Once again this reinforces the whole-person perspective. An attentive and mutually supportive relationship with your life partner will have a positive impact on your working experiences. If you are female, there is firm evidence that being fully engaged in a rich family life is likely to increase your work engagement (Rothbard, 2001). When you have close family relationships that matter enormously to you, feeling content and happy about them will obviously have an impact on your state, which will carry over into your work interactions and reactions. For too long we have treated work and family experiences in a professional context as if they were happening to different people. For example, if one of your team at work is suffering from stress you are quite likely to be encouraged by HR to find out if it is caused by work or home factors. It is probable that both will be having a causal influence and trying to suggest it has to be one or the other could be misleading and result in taking only a partial approach to the issues. The more our lines between work and the rest of our lives become blurred the greater the extent to which the quality of home and work relationships cross over in terms of their impact. Investing in building and maintaining good relationships away from work will have a real impact on the effectiveness of the relationships you have as a middle manager.

This also links to the need to not get too self-absorbed. Believing life is all about you doesn't seem to do you any good in the long term. It increases the likelihood of readily adopting a victim mindset and ultimately damaging your psychological resilience. Having an outlook on life that is in part about making a positive impact on other people's lives seems to have shared benefits for others and for you. Tied to this is the capacity to freely express gratitude. Taken together it seems to us that an open, empathetic and appreciative approach to others is important in maintaining a healthy psychological balance between your needs and other people's. Having this approach to relationships away from work is very likely to permeate your approach to work relationships.

Seeking and embracing tough challenges

Cruising along permanently in your comfort zone is a recipe for boredom, reduced learning, and ultimately dissatisfaction. In our experience middle managers who are resilient and effective in the long term not only accept tough challenges but seek them. This is true at work and is linked to continuing to develop in your career; however, it is likely to hold in all areas of life. Of course what constitutes a tough challenge is ultimately fairly subjective. We are not necessarily advocating you need to seek adrenalin rush experiences. Essentially anything that stretches you and demands that you adapt your typical behavioural patterns and learn new skills can be a tough experience. This stretch may be purely psychological or have a physical component. If you have never run a marathon you will certainly need to train to build your physical endurance, but anyone who has done one will tell you that psychological resilience is at least as important, and possibly more so.

Learning something new is almost certainly good for you cognitively, particularly as you age, but real challenges often make emotional demands. For many of us thinking about deliberately challenging ourselves emotionally is much less intuitive than doing so physically or cognitively. It is more likely that you start by focusing on the latter aspects of the challenge but find the emotional stretch along the way. For example, say you decide you want to master a new language. This is mainly a knowledge challenge but you will need the emotional resilience to persevere when, as is probably inevitable, you find some aspects of the language particularly difficult to get to grips with. If after a year you are asked what you have achieved, you will almost certainly focus on your new language knowledge and skills. It would be quite unusual to start by mentioning that you learnt to deal better emotionally with disappointments and setbacks, and to control the negative emotions that may prevent you trying to speak when you are far from mastering the language. However, in many ways this may be the most important thing you have learnt.

Some people do choose new life challenges that they know will be very emotionally demanding, such as volunteering as a bereavement counsellor or undertaking support activities with seriously ill children. Clearly these are often admirable choices, but need more consideration in terms of the impact they will have on you than undertaking something like learning Chinese Mandarin or how to play the piano. Of course many who undertake such emotionally demanding activity find it inherently satisfying and rewarding. In doing so they experience deep positive emotions that can counterbalance some raw negative ones along the way. Ultimately, you may feel you are not at the right stage in your life to take on such emotionally demanding voluntary work. Nevertheless, considering the emotional side of challenge is important, rather than just focusing on acquiring new knowledge and skills or overcoming a physical challenge.

There are probably combination challenges that are most likely to enhance your overall wellbeing, resilience and life satisfaction. These would have the following components:

- acquiring new knowledge;
- learning a new skill;
- social;
- making a contribution to the happiness or wellbeing of others;
- caring for the environment or long-term sustainability of humanity;
- emotional stretch.

Trying to find a challenge that encompasses all of the above may well be your biggest challenge! Possibly something like working with underprivileged people to carry out countryside maintenance work would come close. In practice, engineering the challenges you take on to fit all of the above criteria probably isn't the most important point here. It is about adopting an approach to life where you continue to challenge yourself in different areas and throughout your lifespan. Naturally this needs to be managed against the other work and broader life demands you face. For most of us there are times in our life when the thought of deliberately seeking a new challenge is beyond what we could cope with, and this is a natural part of the lifecycle. However, if it has been a number of years since you felt truly stretched the time may be right to seek a different opportunity to challenge yourself.

Living a mindful life

Mindfulness has been growing rapidly in popularity both in business and related to general wellbeing. At its core, mindfulness is purposeful and concentrated attention: 'Mindfulness means paying attention in a particular way; on purpose, in the present moment, and nonjudgmentally' (Kabat-Zinn, 2012).

Mindfulness, which has its origins in Buddhist traditions, usually manifests in the form of meditation-like exercises. There is growing evidence that mindfulness-based stress reduction (MBSR) and cognitive therapy (MBCT) can have positive health benefits, particularly in terms of reducing cardio-vascular disease risks (Abbott *et al*, 2014). In a work context the benefits seem to include reducing emotional exhaustion and improving job satisfaction (Hülsheger *et al*, 2013).

In our increasingly busy lives it is not surprising that mindfulness is proving very popular in many businesses and organizations. There is so much activity noise (and middle managers are often in the loudest spot), and finding techniques that help to turn this down to concentrate are very valuable. However, we need to be careful that we are not looking to mindfulness as another quick fix or magic bullet solution. Perhaps reducing some of the noise is a better long-term solution than providing everyone with mindfulness training? In practice, as with many of the organizational challenges we face, it is optimal to consider coming at this from both angles. Controlling the noise in our lives is a good idea, not least because it will probably have a direct impact on others such as your team at work, or your family at home. However, using mindfulness or related techniques that help us to focus better, and which rejuvenate us by practising them, also makes a lot of sense.

The principles of mindfulness can be beneficial when applied beyond individual meditation. Interpersonal mindfulness is about being fully present and engaged with others. One interesting idea is the notion that being mindful with others provides enhanced response flexibility. Rather than just responding to situations in a knee-jerk habitual way, by having a heightened awareness of what is happening in a situation you increase your ability to consciously choose your response. Glomb *et al* (2011) suggest that there is a growing body of evidence linking mindfulness practice to response flexibility. This is clearly a useful capacity to develop, both for relationships at home and work. For example, imagine you arrive home after a difficult day at work (assuming you have those occasionally) and your partner who has been at home on a day's holiday asks you to do the cooking. Rather than allowing a possibly irritated reaction to immediately surface, you choose a more appropriate response! This is more likely if you have the capacity to mindfully attend to the situation you are now in, rather than reacting almost entirely on the basis of the one you have left behind.

Mindful team interactions would be those where the participants are fully focused on what is happening in the interaction they are currently having. They are not distracted by smart phones or the work they think they should be doing, but fully present and attentive for their colleagues. Perhaps more regular adoption of such practices would actually shorten team meetings and make them more productive? Glomb and her colleagues also highlight a link between mindfulness practice and increased empathy, which is relevant here. Being fully present for others makes it much easier to see the world through their eyes. The more we rush from meeting to meeting, continually crisis manage, and half-focus on what we are doing alongside thinking about what we need to do next, the less likely we are to empathize with others and truly understand their perspective.

We are not arguing that you need to be constantly mindful. Given this is a state of enhanced concentration it may be far too difficult to sustain constantly. In addition, there are times when you need to react quickly, knowing that you have not fully appreciated the nuances of the current situation. However, being able to switch into a mindful state from time to time could be a significant asset for you and the people you regularly interact with. If your organization introduces mindfulness, or if you try to bring it in, we suggest considering what you can gain from it collectively, not just individually. Meditation practices may be a good starting point, but considering how you can adopt mindful team practices could take the intervention to the next level in terms of the impact it has.

Living to work and working to live

To be an outstanding middle manager this isn't a choice you need to make. You need to do both. If you are not at some level living to work, you will be disengaged, unhappy and unfulfilled in your mid-level role. If you are not working to live you may be becoming too insular and work obsessed to the extent that you neglect other areas of your life. Taking a whole-person perspective where you recognize that your work needs to be a meaningful and fulfilling part of an even more meaningful and fulfilling life seems to us essential to sustaining a successful and rewarding mid-level career. We suggest you reflect on the areas covered in this chapter and link them to what you have learnt from the earlier parts of this book. To support you to do this, the final chapter is designed to help you fully capture and integrate what you have gained from reading this book, in a way that will help you identify actions that will improve your working and life experience.

Becoming an outstanding middle manager

09

In this chapter we review what we have covered in the book as a whole. The main purpose of the chapter is to help you to consolidate what you have learnt from the book and to identify actions that can support you in your career and life goals. We suggest actions that may enable you to form your own action plan. We complete the chapter by highlighting the areas we feel those responsible for leadership and management development could fruitfully focus on to develop outstanding middle managers.

In the opening chapter of this book we argued that there is a need to reconsider and reframe middle management. We have tried to build the case that managing in the middle, particularly in large organizations, is critically important and often enormously undervalued. If that is where you operate now then it is feasible that you will continue to work in the middle for a substantial part of your remaining career, and perhaps all of it. That should not be a thought that fills you with despair although, if you are currently struggling with mid-level pressures, your current experience may tip your initial reaction in that direction. However, you can build a satisfying and influential career at middle management level. Of course you can get lost in the middle but you can also be outstanding there.

We don't want to give the impression that becoming an outstanding middle manager is just about management. We have argued that management has been devalued in comparison to leadership over the last 30 years or so. Nevertheless, leadership is important. You should lead as a middle manager. Setting direction and motivating people to go there with passion and purpose should be part of your role. However, the value you can uniquely add is to lead with a full understanding and mastery of the realities of managing to ultimately achieve real progress. It is also likely that there are important parts of your role that do not involve leading or managing. You may be a senior specialist, for example a head of finance or IT, where you need to regularly use your high level of expertise to make an important contribution. In fact, for many it makes sense to think about the relative balance you need to achieve between leading, managing and working in your specialist or technical domain.

Generally, we are arguing that management has been devalued and should actually be seen as the most important part (assuming you are in a mid-level role). To illustrate this, imagine you head a function in a large organization, reporting to executive level. If that's where you are already you won't need to imagine too hard. Table 9.1 suggests what might result with various blends of leadership, management and specialist focus.

We are not arguing that the percentage splits in the table are completely accurate. We are suggesting that in this type of role, management activity should take up the majority of your time and focus, irrespective of your job title. This is where you can be outstanding. It can also be where you can gain true fulfilment and purpose. The idea that management, particularly in comparison to leadership, is boring and unexciting is one we would challenge. Of course there are aspects of management activity that can become tedious and repetitive. However, what's boring about playing the core role in seeing an organization realize its ambitions by transforming strategy into operational reality? What's boring about spending time and energy truly enabling your team to perform at their best and working in a real partnership with senior leaders? Good leadership sets up the conditions for these activities; good management delivers them.

Table 9.1   Potential activity mix consequences for a functional head

Orientation	Results
60% Leadership 20% Management 20% Specialist work	Direction set and time taken to try to motivate and energize people towards following. However, implementation of change becomes disorganized and weak. Activity often chaotic. Those at the level below end up confused and unconvinced that goals are achievable due to poor resourcing, planning and organization. Crisis management becomes the default operational state. Senior executives are initially positive in seeing mirrors of themselves, but gradually realize the management input they require to achieve their goals is missing. Management activity becomes misunderstood and under-valued.
60% Specialist work 20% Management 20% Leadership	Technical/specialist excellence. However, the management and development of resources (particularly people) is weak. Operates almost like an academic function rather than a business or operational one. The real impact of specialist expertise in terms of practical value add gets lost. Management, and people leadership, are seen as intellectually inferior.
60% Management 20% Leadership 20% Specialist work	Unique value added. Turning strategic goals into practical reality. Connected effectively in all directions by being fully engaged in the day-to-day reality of operational life. Able to spot implementation flaws, and well-informed new opportunities, in strategic intent. Protecting enough time for leadership and specialist work to maintain balance in the role and reducing the risk of getting lost in the constant operational pressures and noise of mid-level activity.

Figure 9.1 Goal capture framework

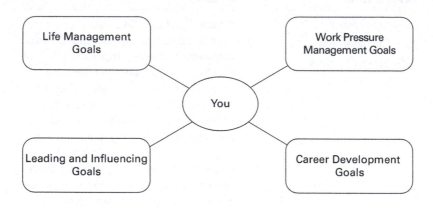

Converting goals into actions

At the end of Chapter 1 we encouraged you to capture your goals using the framework illustrated in Figure 9.1. We would now like to try to help you convert these into actions by drawing on what we hope you have taken from this book. Below we suggest specific actions linked to this framework. You may find they closely match your needs and context, and decide to adopt them as they are expressed here. It is more likely that you will need to modify them and make them your own by tailoring them to your unique circumstances. You may decide to completely disregard them and draw up your own independent set of actions. Any of those options represents progress. The critical point is that you do some action planning based on what you have taken from the book. Otherwise, to paraphrase an old proverb, your road to hell may be paved with your best intentions.

Work pressure management goals

The starting point for ensuring you stay on top of your work pressures is to think again about the pressure you put yourself under. You need to accept that you are not perfect and won't be able to do everything perfectly. If you recognize a strong perfectionist streak in your character you need to learn to control the pressure that will result. Having high standards and expectations is a very positive quality: it drives high performance and usually means you will try to take control of difficult situations and find a solution. However, beating yourself up endlessly because you haven't reached a probably unachievable standard really is wasted energy, as well as being self-induced stress. Having ambitious goals is fine but you should expect setbacks along the way, and accept that you may have to reshape your goals as you work towards them. Below are a number of suggested actions.

Action 1

If you 'suffer' from perfectionism our first suggested action is: identify three current work challenges where you will accept a solution that reaches 80 per cent of what you consider to be a perfect outcome. Write down a summary of what 80 per cent success looks like and ensure you move on when this is obtained.

Depending on what you do there may be some activities that do need to be perfect. For example, if you are responsible for signing off the annual management accounts before they go to the board you may not want to try the 80 per cent rule here. The point in part is being able to differentiate between what needs to be perfect and what is perfectly acceptable. Don't consistently waste time you don't have overengineering the last 20 per cent, when it is in an area that makes no difference to anyone but you.

Action 2

The second suggested action is linked to ensuring you do all you can to manage your time optimally. The only way to do this consistently well is to have clarity about your key work and life goals. Scanning all of the goals you identified at the end of Chapter 1, in the light of your thinking having read this book, is a strong starting point. There are two suggested actions here. One is related to the importance of keeping a broad whole-person orientation and the second to recognizing the need to say no.

Capture the three or four main life goals you have for the next three years and list the work activities that are key to supporting these. Actively review this as a habitual 'start the week' activity.

Action 3

Write down two or three activities you believe you regularly get involved in that are low to medium priority. For the next two weeks say no to any attempt to involve you in these unless someone truly convinces you of the need to be involved. Create a 'To don't' list.

The point with Action 2 is to actively and regularly stay oriented towards what really matters to you in life, not just the screaming, immediate demands of work. The point with Action 3 is to practise thinking about and reacting to requests for your time by referencing what you should and probably shouldn't get involved with. If your personality means you find it difficult to say no, practising doing so is important, even though it goes against the grain. If this is less of a problem for you, thinking about what you tend to get drawn into that you probably shouldn't is still a useful exercise. You should learn to say no politely but assertively, if you have not already done so.

Overall it is worth spending some time reviewing the work demands you face and thinking about where you may need to take a more active or different approach to managing them.

Career development goals

In Chapter 4 we set out a tool for career planning, based on the structure in Figure 9.2 and we won't repeat ourselves here. However, it is worth reviewing this and pulling out your main action in each area.

Figure 9.2 Structuring your career development

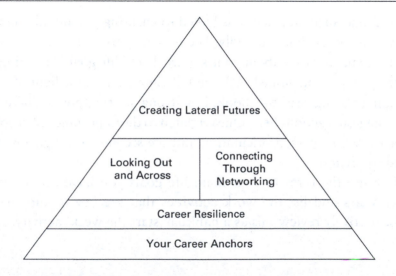

There are a number of meta-questions that may help you to get to what you most need to do first:

- Career anchors – Do you understand your main career anchors and what they suggest for your career and life goals?

- Career resilience – Can you identify where you need to be out of your comfort zone to develop your career and what you need to do to cope in such periods?

- Looking out and across/Connecting through networking – Do you have a clear networking strategy and plan, and devote sufficient time to implementing it?

- Creating lateral futures – Do you have a flexible but clear career development plan with core goals, with scope for path changes in working towards those goals?

Action 4

Essentially we have a broad single action to suggest here: find two hours in the next two weeks to review your career development goals and strategy. Create an action plan using the structure suggested above.

The most important aspect here is regularly finding time to think about, and work on, your career development. This is something that can easily drift and only be actively engaged in once or twice a year around appraisal time. Your career surely merits more frequent consideration.

Leading and influencing goals

This covers influencing in all directions: upwards, downwards and sideways. We covered a broad territory here in Chapters 5, 6 and 7. In Chapter 5 we introduced the team confidence builder, which may be something you decide to include in your work with your team.

Action 5

The core action we propose with your team is: capture the development activity you have undertaken with your team to date and its impact. Identify where you believe there are still performance gaps and formulate options for addressing these within the next six months.

Action 6

In Chapter 6 we discussed influencing your peers at the same or similar level to you. This included encouragement to consider your influencing goals at close and distant proximity to you. Of the three directions of influence we discuss in the book, sideways influence is the least likely to be supported by existing organizational structures and processes. Therefore, a key starting point is to consider how you can build supporting mechanisms for enhanced regular peer networking.

Identify the mechanisms you can use, or build, to enhance your peer networking (eg peer mentoring, initiating a regular peer meeting structure). Find some peers you trust to discuss this with and seek to recruit them to help you better utilize or establish new peer networking structures or processes.

Action 7

In Chapter 7 we focused on influencing upwards, particularly through the relationship you have with your boss. The action you need to take here very much depends on the state of this relationship. Therefore, our initial suggestion is that you review this state.

List the positives in your relationship with your manager and the key areas where you believe the relationship could improve. If you have a reasonably healthy relationship with your manager, suggest a discussion based on this. You could ask your boss to make his or her own list before you meet. If you believe your current relationship is dysfunctional or toxic, a more productive starting point may be to identify someone else at the same or more senior level you can have an informal discussion with first.

Life management goals

In the previous chapter we discussed the importance of taking a whole-person approach to becoming, and sustaining a career as, an outstanding middle manager. We concluded this by suggesting that this is best achieved when you both live to work and work to live.

Action 8

So, a good initial action here seems to be: identify where you 'live to work'; specifically, the meaning and purpose you get from work. Also identify where you 'work to live' – what is it that work enables you to do to live a satisfying and fulfilling life beyond the job itself? You may want to discuss what you capture here with your life partner. Return to this from time to time both as a check step for your life priorities, and as a motivator.

In many ways this might be the place to start. Having a well-defined sense of where work fits into your life as a whole is probably the best contextual reference point for identifying other goals and actions.

The ultimate middle management challenge

The ultimate challenge as a middle manager is not managing in the middle of the pressure sandwich between senior management and the levels below. It is not ensuring your career is progressing and motivating. It is not even managing the demands of work and the rest of your life to find a sustainable balance or integration. These are all ingredients, but the ultimate middle management challenge is continuously managing the four key areas outlined above that flow from Figure 9.1. It is so easy to get immersed in today's priorities and spend little or no time stepping away from them to consider the bigger picture. The busier we get in work and life the more difficult this becomes and, conversely, the more important it is. Ensuring you devote time to regularly step away from the day-to-day minutiae and take this broad integrative perspective is crucial to your survival and growth in middle management. Adopt whatever strategy works for you to achieve this. You may want to try the mnemonic CLIP (Career, Lifestyle, Influencing, Pressures) as a way of frequently cueing yourself into this process.

We are not seeking to raise your anxiety levels by encouraging you to reflect frequently on these broad areas with the result that you get worried that you are not addressing them all as well as you would like. A key thought here is that we need to reflect broadly because life is *never* static and perfect. Don't reflect with the view that everything should be in perfect harmony and progressing towards the middle management nirvana! Life is much too complex and dynamic for that to be the reality for any length of time. Use mindfulness principles here. Just be mindful about a broader range of influences and factors that need to be managed. Raised awareness and concentration do not need to result in raised stress levels – acceptance is important here. In fact, there is a particular mindfulness-related therapeutic approach, ACT (Acceptance and Commitment Therapy), which has at its core the principle we are advocating here. The basis is to accept rather than avoid, or necessarily control, the factors that matter and then commit to the best course of action. So, for example, accepting that your career may not be progressing is different from avoiding that thought. Having accepted it you can go on to identify the best course of action to move towards your goals and commit to a path that may take you there from where you are now.

In practice there usually needs to be a balance between acceptance and control, which is still represented best by The Serenity Prayer: 'God, grant me the serenity to accept the things I cannot change, courage to change the things I can, and wisdom to know the difference' (Niebuhr, c. 1932). The essential aspect here is paying attention from time to time to the broad range of important influences on you as a middle manager, and not just the immediate; then better controlling what you can, accepting what you have limited or no control over, and committing to the next steps you need to take to achieve your most important goals.

Developing middle managers

You may be reading this as someone who has responsibility for leadership and/or management development in a business or organization, rather than as a middle manager. We believe there are certain lessons from this book that could be applied to improve the development of those in mid-level roles. These include:

1 the need to balance leadership and management development;

2 pressure management development;

3 supporting lateral career development; and

4 developing the whole person.

1. Balancing leadership and management development

We have argued that for those in mid-level positions, management is at least as important as leadership in terms of their core role. In our view this should be reflected in the development people in these roles are exposed to. We are certainly not suggesting that leadership development should be off the agenda; people at these levels should lead. However, they should receive more good quality management development, focusing on core management skills such as planning, organizing, time management, resource allocation, project management and budgeting.

The area where there is probably most cross-over between leadership and management is leading/managing people. In our view this is often where mixing both perspectives is useful. For example, take the Kouzes and Posner (2007) leadership practices (largely people leadership oriented) we introduced in Chapter 7 and consider some of their possible people management implications (see Table 9.2). The reality of people leadership and management seems so intertwined that separating these developmentally may be somewhat artificial.

2. Pressure management development

We believe that people in mid-level roles in large organizations are exposed to more pressures, and a wider range of them, than virtually any other group. Of course there is work and life pressure for everyone, regardless of level. However, development focused on helping middle managers better cope with and actively manage the unique blend of pressures they face should pay dividends. This includes sandwich organizational pressures as well as the broader life pressures likely to be experienced by the generation that predominates at mid-levels.

3. Supporting lateral career development

Does your organization do enough to support employees in the middle to continue to develop their careers without necessarily getting a hierarchical promotion? For example, are development projects identified that expose middle managers to very different functions and processes?

Table 9.2 Leadership practices and people management implications

Leadership practice (Kouzes and Posner, 2007)	People management implication
Model the way	Need to understand how what you do to model the way is interpreted and implemented by others. This can be assessed through processes such as performance management.
Inspire a shared vision	A forum may be required to discuss and agree this shared vision with your team. It will need to be managed in terms of how and when it is discussed and how outputs are captured.
Challenge the process	To credibly challenge a process, you need evidence that the existing one is not optimal and that there is a better alternative. This might require a team project to establish this and capture supporting data.
Enable others to act	There will be a need to clarify where others are fully empowered and where they aren't: this needs planning and management.
Encourage the heart	Probably needs least management! However, being emotionally inspired still needs to ultimately result in well channelled and organized activity.

A formal peer mentoring scheme might be a helpful intervention here. It is also worth considering whether there are rewards available to people who do all they can to develop laterally, other than the intrinsically motivating ones that come from doing so.

4. Developing the whole person

Initiatives that seek to support employees to develop as healthy, balanced and rounded individuals that have little or no obvious direct work relevance can have a number of advantages. One is to enhance your employer brand as an organization that truly values your people beyond their direct human resource value (although you will get gains there). If these are linked to environmental or charitable work, so much the better. This tends to have benefits for employee well-being and the image of the organization or business. This area isn't, and shouldn't be, unique to middle managers. However, mid-level individuals will often be at a life stage where they are seeking broader meaning. This may just be a mid-life crisis, or a more positive need to ensure that they can connect to a broader purpose and understand at a deeper level how what they do for a living fits with this purpose.

So be outstanding

Positively reframing the role you play as a middle manager is likely to be very good for you, your business or organization, and your family and friends. We have been through waves of hierarchical top-down management, and upside-down management (led from the front line); perhaps it is time for positive management from the middle. Making the middle the outstanding level in your organization may be the transformational programme that no one has tried yet. Middle managers can and should stand out. It's a cliché, but they truly are the glue that can hold the organization together.

If you are a middle manager we hope that you have found this book positive, insightful and practical. We hope you can use some of what you have learnt from it to become outstanding in what you do, and healthier and more fulfilled in your life as a whole.

REFERENCES

Abbott, R A, Whear, R, Rodgers, L R, Bethel, A, Thompson Coon, J, Kuyken, W, Stein, K and Dickens, C (2014) Effectiveness of mindfulness-based stress reduction and mindfulness based cognitive therapy in vascular disease: a systematic review and meta-analysis of randomised controlled trials, *Journal of Psychosomatic Research*, 76, pp 341–51

Accenture (2007) *Press release: Middle managers around the world unsatisfied with their organizations, Accenture survey finds*, New York

Allen, C, Bearg, N, Foley, R and Smith, J (2011) *Reboot Your Life: Energize your career and life by taking a break*, Beaufort Books, New York

Antoncic, B and Hisrich, R D (2001) Intrapreneurship: Construct refinement and cross-cultural validation, *Journal of Business Venturing*, 16, pp 495–527

APA (2014) *Stress in America*, The American Psychological Association, annual report, APA, Washington, DC

Bajkowski, J (2015) All change, pressure on the public sector, Culture Management, http://www.governmentnews.com.au/2015/01/all-change-pressure-on-the-public-sector/ [accessed 11.04.16]

Bakker, A B, Van Veldhoven, M and Xanthopoulou, D (2010) Beyond the demand-control model: thriving on high job demands and resources, *Journal of Personnel Psychology*, 9 (1), pp 3–16

Bañares Parera, I and Fernández-Vallejo, A M (2013) Changes in the role of middle manager: a historical point of view, *International Journal of Information and Education Technology*, 3 (3)

Bandura, A (2000) Exercise of human agency through collective efficacy, *Current Directions in Psychological Science*, 9 (3), pp 75–8

Bank Workers Charity (2013) *Bank on Your People: The state of wellbeing and high performance culture in the financial sector*, The Bank Workers Charity, London

Barber, B (2011) Lean and its Impact on Employee Empowerment within a Higher Education Institution, unpublished dissertation, Pepperdine University, Malibu, CA

Barley, S R, Meyerson, D E and Grodal, S (2011) E-mail as a source and symbol of stress, *Organizational Science*, 22 (4), pp 887–906

Belbin, R M (2010) *Team Roles at Work*, Routledge, Taylor & Francis, London

Bevan, S (2012) *Good Work, High Performance and Productivity*, The Work Foundation, London

Boddy, C R (2011) Corporate psychopaths, bullying and unfair supervision in the workplace, *Journal of Business Ethics*, **100** (3)

Boddy, C R, Ladyshewsky, R and Galvin, P (2010) Leaders without ethics in global business: corporate psychopaths, *Journal of Public Affairs*, **10** (3), pp 121–38

Boston Consulting Group (2010) Creating a new deal for middle managers. Empowering a neglected but critical group, http://www.bcg.com/documents/file52425.pdf [accessed 09.04.16]

Bourne, L and Walker, D H T (2005) Visualising and mapping stakeholder influence, *Management Decision*, **43** (5), pp 649–60

Bowling, N A, Beehr, T A and Swader, W M (2005) Giving and receiving social support at work: the roles of personality and reciprocity, *Journal of Vocational Behavior*, **67** (3), pp 476–89

Brown, N J L, Sokal, A D and Friedman, H L (2013) The complex dynamics of wishful thinking: the critical positivity ratio, *American Psychologist*, **68**, July

Bryant, S E (2005) The impact of peer mentoring on organizational knowledge creation and sharing, *Group Organization Management*, **30** (3), pp 319–38

Buckingham, M and Coffman, C (1999) *First, Break All the Rules: What great managers do differently*, Simon & Schuster, London

BUPA (2013) Managers too stressed to notice junior staff struggle, http://www.bupa.com/media-centre/press-releases/uk/22-nov-2013-managers-too-stressed-to-notice-junior-staff-struggle/ [accessed 30.03.15]

Buysse, D J (2014) Sleep health: can we define it? Does it matter? *Sleep*, **37** (1), pp 917

Carlson, D S, Hunter, E M, Ferguson, M and Whitten, D (2011) Work-family enrichment and satisfaction: mediating processes and relative impact of originating and receiving domains, *Journal of Management*, **40** (3), pp 845–65

Caye, J-M, Strack, R, Orlander, P, Kilman, J, Espinosa, E G, Francouer, F and Haen, P (2010) *Creating a New Deal for Middle Managers: Empowering a neglected but critical group*, The Boston Consulting Group, World Federation of People Management Associations, Boston MA

Cerdin, J L and Le Pargneux, M (2010) Career anchors: a comparison between organization-assigned and self-initiated expatriates, *Thunderbird International Business Review*, **52** (4), pp 287–99

Chang, C L H, Jiang, J J, Klein, G and Chen, H G (2012) Career anchors and disturbances in job turnover decisions – a case study of IT professionals in Taiwan, *Information & Management*, 49 (6), pp 309–19

CIPD (2005) *Bullying at Work: Beyond policies to a culture of respect,* Chartered Institute of Personnel and Development, London

CIPD (2012) *Leading Culture Change: Employee engagement and public service transformation,* Chartered Institute of Personnel and Development, London

CIPD (2014) *Are We Working Harder Than Ever?* Chartered Institute of Personnel and Development, London

Coats, D (2006) An agenda for work: The Work Foundation's challenge to policy makers, Provocation Series, 1 (2), The Work Foundation, London

Coetzee, M and Schreuder, D (2011) The relation between career anchors, emotional intelligence and employability satisfaction among workers in the service industry, *Southern African Business Review*, 15 (3), pp 76–97

Cooke-Davies, T J (2005) The executive sponsor: the hinge upon which organisational project management maturity turns, *Proceedings of PMI Global Congress*, PM Institute, Edinburgh

Cooperrider, D L, Whitney, D and Stavros, J M (2008) *Appreciative Inquiry Handbook: For leaders of change,* 2nd edn, Crown Custom Publishing, Brunswick, OH

Costa, P T and McCrae, R R (1992) *Revised NEO Personality Inventory (NEO PI-R) and NEO Five-Factor Inventory (NEO-FFI),* Psychological Assessment Resources, Odessa, FL

Covey, S R (1992) *The Seven Habits of Highly Effective People*, Simon & Schuster, London

Crace, R K and Brown, D (1996) *Life Values Inventory,* Life Values Resources, Chapel Hill, NC

Cummings, S and Angwin, D (2004) The future shape of strategy: lemmings or chimeras? *Academy of Management Executive*, 18 (2), pp 21–36

Currie, G and Procter, S (2005) The antecedents of middle managers' strategic contribution: the case of a professional bureaucracy, *Journal of management studies,* 42, pp 1325–56

Direnzo, M S, Greenhaus, J and Weer, C H (2015) Relationship between protean career orientation and work-life balance: a resource perspective, *Journal of Organizational Behavior,* 36, pp 538–60

Dopson, S and Stewart, R (1990) What is happening to middle management, *British Journal of Management*, 1, pp 3–16

Dowling, M and Lucey, B (2014) From hubris to nemesis: Irish banks, behavioral biases, and the crisis, *Journal of Risk Management in Financial Institutions*, 7 (2)

Edwards, K (2013) Monkey study reveals why middle managers suffer the most stress, http://www.manchester.ac.uk/discover/news/article/?id=9783 [accessed 10.04.16]

Englund, R L and Bocero, A (2006) *Project Sponsorship*, Jossey-Bass, San Francisco, CA

Erez, M, Lisak, A, Harush, R, Glikson, E, Nouri, R and Shokef, E (2013) Going global: developing management students' cultural intelligence and global identity in culturally diverse virtual teams, *Academy of Management Learning & Education*, **12** (3), pp 330–55

Erickson, T (2010) *What's Next Gen X?* Harvard Business Press, Boston, MA

European Commission (2013) *Quality of Life in Europe: Subjective wellbeing,* Publications Office of the European Union, Luxembourg

Flint-Taylor, J and Robertson, I (2007) Leaders' impact on well-being and performance: an empirical test of a model, Paper presented at the British Psychological Society, Division of Occupational Psychology, Annual Conference, Bristol, January

Floyd, S and Woodridge, B (1994) Dinosaurs or dynamos? Recognizing middle management's strategic role, *Academy of Management Executive*, **8** (4), pp 47–57

Fredrickson, B (2009) *Positivity: Groundbreaking research to release your inner optimist and thrive,* Oneworld Publications, London

Fredrickson, B L and Cohn, M A (2008) Positive emotions, in (eds) M Lewis, J Haviland and L F Barrett, *Handbook of Emotions,* 3rd edn, Guilford Press, New York, pp 777–96

French, J P R and Raven, B (1960) The bases of social power, in (eds) D Cartwright and A Zander, *Group Dynamics*, Harper and Row, New York, pp 607–23

Gabarro, J J and Kotter, J P (2005) Managing your boss, *Harvard Business Review,* January

Glomb, T M, Duffy, M K, Bono, J E and Yang, T (2011) Mindfulness at work, in (eds) Aparna Joshi, Hui Liao and Joseph J Martocchio, *Research in Personnel and Human Resources Management* (Vol 30) Emerald Group Publishing Limited, pp 115–57

Gratton, L (2012) The end of the middle manager, https://hbr.org/2011/01/column-the-end-of-the-middle-manager [accessed 10.04.16]

Greenhaus, J H and Powell, G N (2006) When work and family are allies: theory of work-family enrichment, *Academy of Mangement Review*, **31** (1), pp 72–92

Greenhaus, J H and Powell, G N (2012) The family-relatedness of work decisions: a framework and agenda for theory and research, *Journal of Vocational Behavior, 80,* pp 246–55

Gruber, M J, Gelman, B D and Ranganath, C (2014) States of curiosity modulate hippocampus-dependent learning via dopaminergic circuit, *Neuron*, 84 (2), pp 486–96

Gujar, N, Yoo, S-S, Hu, P and Walker, M P (2011) Sleep deprivation amplifies reactivity of brain reward networks, biasing the appraisal of positive emotional experiences, *Journal of Neuroscience*, 31 (12), pp 4464–74

Hannon, K (2012) 6 key steps for career resilience, http://www.forbes.com/sites/kerryhannon/2012/12/26/6-key-steps-for-career-resilience/ [accessed 10.04.16]

Harvard Business School (2015) Program for leadership development, http://www.exed.hbs.edu/programs/pld/Pages/default.aspx [accessed 10.04.16]

Hassard, J, Morris, J and McCann, L (2012) My brilliant career? New organizational forms and changing managerial careers in Japan, the UK, and USA, *Journal of Management Studies*, 49 (3)

Health and Safety Executive (2012) What are the management standards? http://www.hse.gov.uk/stress/standards/ [accessed 10.04.16]

Higgins, C A, Judge, T A and Ferris, G R (2003) Influence tactics and work outcomes: a meta-analysis, *Journal of Organizational Behavior*, 24, pp 89–106

Hobsbawm, J (2014) Networking – it's who you know, HR Magazine, December, http://www.hrmagazine.co.uk/hr/features/1148575/networking [accessed 10.04.16]

Hofstede, G (2001) *Culture's Consequences: Comparing values, behaviors, institutions, and organizations across nations*, Sage, Thousand Oaks, CA

Hülsheger, U R, Alberts, H J E M, Feinholdt, A and Lang, J W B (2013) Benefits of mindfulness at work: the role of mindfulness in emotion regulation, emotional exhaustion, and job satisfaction, *Journal of Applied Psychology*, 98 (2), pp 310–25

Jackson, M L, Gunzelmann, G, Whitney, P, Hinson, J M, Belenky, G, Rabat, A and Van Dongen, H P A (2013) Deconstructing and reconstructing cognitive performance in sleep deprivation, *Sleep Med Rev*, 17 (3), pp 215–25

Jones, R, Latham, J and Betta, M (2013) Creating the illusion of employee empowerment: lean production in the international automobile industry, *The International Journal of Human Resource Management*, 24 (8), pp 1629–45

Kabat-Zinn, J (2012) *Mindfulness for Beginners: Reclaiming the present moment – and your life*, Sounds True, Colorado

Kaplan, R S and Norton, D P (1992) The balanced scorecard: measures that drive performance, *Harvard Business Review*, January–February, pp 71–9

Kelley, R E (2008) Rethinking followership, in (eds) Riggio *et al*, *The Art of Followership*, Jossey-Bass, San Francisco, CA

Kelly, G (1963) *A Theory of Personality: The psychology of personal constructs*, Norton & Company, New York

Knowledge@Wharton (2005) Clash of the Titans: when top executives don't get along with the team, http://knowledge.wharton.upenn.edu/article/clash-of-the-titans-when-top-executives-dont-get-along-with-the-team/ [accessed 10.04.16]

Kotov, R, Gamez, W, Schmidt, F and Watson, D (2010) Linking 'big' personality traits to anxiety, depressive, and substance use disorders: a meta-analysis, *Psychological Bulletin*, **136** (5), pp 768–821

Kouzes, J M and Posner, B Z (2007) *The Leadership Challenge*, Jossey-Bass, San Francisco, CA

KPMG (2014) War for talent – time to change direction, KPMG International Cooperative, https://www.kpmg.com/Global/en/IssuesAndInsights/ArticlesPublications/war-for-talent/Documents/war-for-talent.pdf [accessed 10.04.16]

Lamm, H (1988) A review of our research on group polarisation: eleven experiments on the effects of group discussion on risk acceptance, probability estimation and negotiation positions, *Psychological Reports*, **62**, pp 807–13

Latham, G P (2004) The motivational benefits of goal-setting, *Academy of Management Executive*, **18** (4)

Leach, D L, Wall, T D, Rogelberg, S G and Jackson, P R (2005) Team autonomy, performance and member job strain: uncovering the teamwork-KSA link, *Applied Psychology: An International Review*, **54** (1), pp 1–24

Legoux, R, Leger, P M, Robert, J and Boyer, M (2014) Confirmation biases in the financial analysis of IT investments, *Journal of the Association for Information Systems*, **15** (1), p 141

LePine, J A, Podsakoff, N P and LePine, M A (2005) A meta-analytic test of the challenge stressor – hindrance stressor framework: an explanation for inconsistent relationships among stressors and performance, *Academy of Management Journal*, **48** (5), pp 764–75

Levinson, J C and Mann, M (2011) *Guerrilla Networking: A proven battle plan to attract the very people you want to meet*, Author House, Bloomington, IN

Locke, E A (1984) *Goal Setting: A motivational technique that works!* Prentice Hall, Englewood Cliffs, NJ

Losada, M and Heaphy, E (2004) The role of positivity and connectivity in the performance of business teams: a nonlinear dynamics model, *American Behavioral Scientist,* **47,** pp 740–65

Luyster, F S, Strollo, P J, Zee, P C and Walsh, J K (2012) Sleep: a health imperative, *Sleep,* **35** (6), pp 727–34

McCallum, J S (2013) Followership: the other side of leadership, *Ivey Business Journal,* September/October

McEvoy, G and Cragun, J R (1997) Using outdoor training to develop and accomplish organizational vision HR, *Human Resource Planning,* **20** (3)

McGregor, D M (1957) *The human side of enterprise,* Management Review, November, pp 41–9

McIntosh, P and Luecke, R A (2011) *Increase Your Influence at Work,* American Management Association, New York

Makin, P, Cooper, C L and Cox, C J (1989) *Managing People at Work,* The British Psychological Society and Routledge, London

Malik, V S, Willett, W C and Hu, F B (2013) Global obesity: trends, risk factors and policy implications, *Nature Reviews Endocrinology,* **9,** January, pp 13–27

Malone, T W (1997) *Is empowerment just a fad? Control, decision making and IT, MIT Sloan Magazine,* http://sloanreview.mit.edu/article/is-empowerment-just-a-fad-control-decision-making-and-it/ [accessed 10.04.16]

Mancuso, V F, Finomore,V S, Rahill, K M, Blair, E A and Funke, G J (2014) Effects of cognitive biases on distributed team decision making, *Proceedings of the Human Factors and Ergonomics Society,* October, Sage Publications, Los Angeles, CA

Mantere, S (2008) Role expectations and middle manager strategic agency, *Journal of Management Studies,* **45** (2), pp 294–316

Marin, J-C (2012) The impact of strategic planning and the balanced scorecard methodology on middle managers' performance in the public sector, *International Journal of Business and Social Science,* **3** (1)

Michaels, E, Handfield-Jones, H and Axelrod, B (2001) *The War for Talent,* Harvard Business School Press, Boston, MA

Migeon, F-D (2011) A duty to modernize: reforming the French civil service, *McKinsey on Government,* Spring

Neal, M B and Hammer, L B (2009) Dual-earner couples in the sandwiched generation: effects of coping strategies over time, *The Psychologist-Manager Journal,* **12,** pp 205–34

Newman, K L and Nollen, S D (1996) Culture and congruence: the fit between management practices and national culture, *Journal of International Business Studies,* **27** (4), pp 753–79

Nickerson, J (2014) *Leading Change from the Middle: A practical guide to building extraordinary capabilities,* Brookings Institution Press, Washington, DC

Nielsen, M B and Einarsen, S (2012) Outcomes of exposure to workplace bullying: a meta-analytic review, *Work & Stress,* **26** (4), pp 309–32

Novak, D, Rennaker, M and Turner, P (2011) Using organizational network analysis to improve integration across organizational boundaries, *People & Strategy,* **34** (4), pp 32–7

O'Reilly, J, Robinson, S L, Berdahl, J F and Bankl, S (2014) Is negative attention better than no attention? The comparative effects of ostracism and harassment at work, *Organization Science,* **26** (3), pp 774–93

Osterman, P (2009) Recognizing the value of middle management, Ivey Business Journal, November/December, http://iveybusinessjournal.com/publication/recognizing-the-value-of-middle-management/ [accessed 04.04.16]

Padilla, A, Hogan, R and Kaiser, R B (2007) The toxic triangle: destructive leaders, susceptible followers, and conducive environments, *The Leadership Quarterly,* **18,** pp 176–94

Pedler, M (2008) *Action Learning for Managers,* Gower, Aldershot

Penedo, F J and Dahn, J R (2005) Exercise and well-being: a review of mental and physical health benefits associated with physical activity, *Current Opinion in Psychiatry: Behavioural Medicine,* **18** (2), pp 189–93

Pepper, A, Gore, J and Crossman, A (2013) Are long-term incentive plans an effective and efficient way of motivating senior executives? *Human Resource Management Journal,* **23** (1), pp 36–51

Peters, S (2012) *The Chimp Paradox: The mind management programme to help you achieve success, confidence and happiness,* Random House Group, London

Pfeffer, J (1992) Understanding power in organizations, *California Management Review,* **34** (2), pp 29–50

Poksinska, B, Swartling, D and Drotz, E (2013) The daily work of Lean leaders: lessons from manufacturing and healthcare, *Total Quality Management,* **24** (8), pp 886–98

Poon, L (2013) Why monkeys in the middle are more stressed, http://news.nationalgeographic.com/news/2013/02/130411-macaque-monkey-stress-middle-manager-hierarchy-behavior-human-science/ [accessed 11.04.16]

Prins, S L, Bates, L M, Keyes, K M and Muntaner, C (2015) Anxious? Depressed? You might be suffering from capitalism: contradictory class locations and the prevalence of depression and anxiety in the USA, *Sociology of Health & Illness*, **37** (8), pp 1352–72

Propst, D B and Koesler, R A (1998) Bandura goes outdoors: role of self-efficacy in the outdoor leadership development process, *Leisure Sciences*, **20** (4)

Raes, A M L, Heijltjes, M G, Glunk, U and Roe, R A (2011) The interface of the top management team and middle managers: a process model, *Academy of Management Review*, **36** (1), pp102–26

Ralston, D A, Lee, C H, Perrewé, P L, Van Deusen, C, Vollmer, G R, Maignan, I, Tang, M, Wan, P and Rossi, A M (2010) A multi-society examination of the impact of psychological resources on stressor-strain relationship, *Journal of International Business Studies*, **41** (4), pp 652–70

Ranganath, C (2014) cited in Durayappah-Harrison, A, The Secret Benefits of a Curious Mind, https://www.psychologytoday.com/blog/thriving101/201410/the-secret-benefits-curious-mind [accessed: 03.06.16]

Rasdi, R M, Ismail, M, Uli, J and Noah, S M (2009) Career aspirations and career success among managers in the Malaysian public sector, *Research Journal of International Studies*, **9**, pp 21–35

Rath, J and Harter, P (2014) *Wellbeing: The five essential elements*, Gallup Press, New York

Robertson Cooper (2010) Uncovering our resilient role models, *Business Wellbeing Network Annual Report*, 24–26

Robertson, I and Cooper, C (2011) *Wellbeing: Productivity and happiness at work*, Palgrave MacMillan, Basingstoke

Roots, C R (1998) *The Sandwich Generation: Adult children caring for aging parents*, Garland Publishing, New York

Rose, K, Shuck, B, Twyford, D and Bergman, M (2015) Skunked: an integrative review exploring the consequences of the dysfunctional leader and implications for those employees who work for them, *Human Resource Development Review*, **1** (27)

Rothbard, N P (2001) The dynamics of engagement in work and family roles, *Administrative Science Quarterly*, **46** (4), pp 655–84

Satell, G (2015) *What makes an organization networked? Harvard Business Review blog*, https://hbr.org/2015/06/what-makes-an-organization-networked?utm_source=Socialflow&utm_medium=Tweet&utm_campaign=Socialflow [accessed 11.04.16]

Schein, E H (1990) *Career Anchors: Discovering your real values*, Pheiffer, San Diego, CA

Schofield, C P (2008) Key challenges facing public sector leaders: themes from Ashridge Public Leadership Centre essay competition 2007, *The Ashridge Journal,* Autumn

Schwarzer, R (2008) Modeling health behavior change: how to predict and modify the adoption and maintenance of health behaviors, *Applied Psychology: An International Review,* 57 (1), pp 1–29

Seligman, M E P (2006) *Learned Optimism: How to change your mind and your life,* Vintage Books, New York

Senge, P M (1990) *The Fifth Discipline: The art & practice of the learning organization,* Doubleday, New York

Siu, O, Spector, P E, Cooper, C L and Lu, L (2005) Work stress, self-efficacy, Chinese work values, and work wellbeing in Hong Kong and Beijing, *International Journal of Stress Management,* 12 (3), pp 274–88

Smeed, M and Tinline, G (2014) Bank on your people: the state of wellbeing and productivity in the financial sector, Bank Workers Charity, http://www.bwcharity.org.uk/sites/default/files/Bank_on_your_people_2014_report.pdf [accessed 11.04.16]

Smith, P (2011) Communication styles as dimensions of national culture, *Journal of Cross-Cultural Psychology,* 42 (2), pp 216–33

Southwick, S M and Charney, D S (2012) *Resilience: The science of mastering life's greatest challenges,* Cambridge University Press, Cambridge

Stoeber, J, Otto, K and Dalbert, C (2009) Perfectionism and the big five: conscientiousness predicts longitudinal increases in self-oriented perfectionism, *Personality and Individual Differences,* 47 (4), pp 363–8

Sull, D, Homkes, R and Sull, C (2015) Why strategy execution unravels – and what to do about it, *Harvard Business Review*, March

Taipale, S, Selander, K, Anttila, T and Natti, J (2011) Work engagement in eight European countries: the role of job demands, autonomy, and social support, *International Journal of Sociology and Social Policy,* 31 (7/8), pp 486–501

Taras, V, Steel, P and Kirkman, B J (2012) Improving national cultural indices using a longitudinal meta-analysis of Hofstede's dimensions, *Journal of World Business,* 47, pp 329–41

The Ladders (2013) Middle management titles are phasing out, http://www.theladders.com/press-releases/theladders-releases-new-job-evolution-data--middle-management-titles-are-phasing-out [accessed 11.04.16]

The Work Foundation (2016) *Good Work overview statement,* http://www.theworkfoundation.com/Research/Workforce-Effectiveness/Good-Work [accessed 11.04.16]

Tversky, A and Kahneman, D (1974) Judgment under uncertainty: heuristics and biases, *Science,* **185,** pp 1124–31

Van Mierlo, H, Rutte, C G, Vermunt, J K, Kompier, M A J and Doorewaard, J A C M (2007) A multi-level mediation model of the relationships between team autonomy, individual task design and psychological well-being, *Journal of Occupational and Organizational Psychology*, **80**, pp 647–64

Vuori, J, Toppinen-Tanner, S and Mutanen, P (2012) Effects of resource-building group intervention on career management and mental health in work organizations: randomized controlled field trial, *Journal of Applied Psychology,* **97** (2), pp 273–86

Waddell, G and Burton, A K (2006) Is work good for your health and well-being? Stationery Office, London, https://www.gov.uk/government/uploads/system/uploads/attachment_data/file/214326/hwwb-is-work-good-for-you.pdf [accessed 11.04.16]

Wall Street Journal (2012) In charts: why middle managers matter, http://blogs.wsj.com/corporate-intelligence/2013/08/06/in-charts-why-middle-managers-matter/ [accessed 11.04.16]

Ward, D (2012) Military innovation in the age of austerity: why I love budget cuts, *National Defense,* **96,** 700 (March)

Wayne, J H, Musisca, N and Fleeson, W (2004) Considering the role of personality in the work-family experience: relationships of the big five to work-family conflict and facilitation, *Journal of Vocational Behavior*, **64**, pp 108–30

Weiner, B (1985) An attributional theory of achievement motivation and emotion, *Psychological Review*, **92** (4), pp 548–73

Wellons, S (2012) The devil in the boardroom: corporate psychopaths and their impact on business, PURE Insights, **1** (1), Article 9, http://digitalcommons.wou.edu/pure/vol1/iss1/9 [accessed 11.04.16]

Wils, L, Wils, T and Tremblay, M (2010) Toward a career anchor structure: an empirical investigation of engineers relations, *Industrielles*, **65** (2) (Spring)

Wulf, J (2012) The flattened firm: not as advertised, *California Management Review*, **55** (1), pp 5–23

INDEX

Note: The index is filed in alphabetical, word-by-word order. Within headings, numbers are filed as spelt out; acronyms are filed as presented. Page locators in *italics* denote information contained within a Figure or Table.

CPSIA information can be obtained
at www.ICGtesting.com
Printed in the USA
LVOW03s2126311016

511028LV00032B/177/P